MW00775423

ADVANCE PRAISE

"Dave Wolcott is one of the best minds in the alternative invest-ment world and in wealth and investing strategy. I am inspired by his mission to help entrepreneurs protect and multiply their wealth and take back control from Wall Street. Dave's holistic approach to wealth building along with the strategies and advice shared in this book will help anyone that is willing to look at money and wealth through a new lens and wants to create a life of abundance and freedom."

—M.C. LAUBSCHER, CREATOR OF CASHFLOW NINJA

"When we get asked what is the #1 most important thing we have learned across forming over 200 family offices, it is to integrate everything, to make sure your values, your team, parts of your balance sheet, your diet, where you live, and what assets you invest in are all aligned and approached holistically. From $10M to $100M to $1B+ net worth clients, the most effective are the most aligned, integrated, and those who play their own unique game in business and in managing their portfolio. This book is a great guide to those who want to be more effective in designing your game board and the rules you will operate by."

—RICHARD C. WILSON, PRESIDENT & FOUNDER OF FAMILY OFFICE CLUB

"*The Holistic Wealth Strategy is a fresh perspective on building personal wealth and financial freedom. Dave's approach starts with developing your 'wealth-building mindset.' This is the core to his proven methodology that enables anyone with the right mindset to separate themselves from Wall Street. Dave's personal experience and pain of following 'Tried and True' traditional stock market investing, which was leaving him financially further behind, pushed him to thoroughly research alternatives. Dave found that his strategy not only worked for him, but works for anyone who wants to get ahead and not follow the pack. Enjoy the book and develop your own wealth-building mindset to create your path to financial success.*"

—GARY MOTTERSHEAD, SERIAL ENTREPRENEUR &
ENTREPRENEURIAL COACH WITH STRATEGIC COACH

"*The Holistic Wealth Strategy is an excellent roadmap for those who want to discover the path to becoming ultra-wealthy and move away from traditional wealth management advice. Dave has a unique knack for taking complex concepts and breaking them down into digestible action steps. If you want to be in the top one percent, then this book is for you.*"

—SAM PRENTICE, CHIEF FINANCIAL
STRATEGIST, WEALTH CEO

"*Dave knocked it out of the park! The Holistic Wealth Strategy is a must-read for any investor who is striving to live a truly free and self-directed life.*"

—HUNTER THOMPSON, MANAGING PRINCIPAL OF ASYM
CAPITAL & FOUNDER OF RAISINGCAPITAL.COM

THE HOLISTIC WEALTH STRATEGY

THE HOLISTIC WEALTH STRATEGY

A Framework for Building Legacy Wealth and Unlimited Freedom to Live an Extraordinary Life

DAVE WOLCOTT

LIONCREST
PUBLISHING

THE HOLISTIC WEALTH STRATEGY
*A Framework for Building Legacy Wealth and
Unlimited Freedom to Live an Extraordinary Life*

FIRST EDITION

ISBN   978-1-5445-3604-0   *Hardcover*
       978-1-5445-3605-7   *Paperback*
       978-1-5445-3606-4   *Ebook*
       978-1-5445-3960-7   *Audiobook*

For my family, Kristine, Adelaide, Claire, John, and Oliver

I dedicate this book to you so you can learn from my mistakes and triumphs to live the life of your dreams.

CONTENTS

INTRODUCTION

When my wife and I had our first child, we realized it was high time to start accelerating our wealth plan. Our best bet, our financial advisors kept telling us, was to continue investing in our company-sponsored 401k plans and establish a college 529 plan. We didn't know any better and had no reason to doubt the experts, so that's exactly what we did. We would have preferred seeing higher returns, but that was what everyone—our parents, our employers, our financial planners—advised. This, we were told, was part of the well-trod path to success that middle-class Americans have been taking for nearly a century.

We then watched our portfolio suffer double-digit significant losses in the 2000 financial crisis. We just felt helpless. We were barely moving the needle with our regular savings efforts and the 7 percent average return from the traditional wealth-building options. It seemed as if our goal number constantly grew bigger while being pushed out further. Retirement, college, and living the life we envisioned were increasingly evasive and cuffed to my wife and me working.

The last straw for me was when our daughter was still a toddler, and we won the baby lottery: we welcomed triplets into our family! Nothing will have you reassessing your wealth plan quite like quadrupling the number of children you have. I developed a nagging feeling that what we were doing financially was just not enough. I always felt that there must be a better way to grow our wealth despite everyone in our lives telling us we were doing the right thing. I wondered: how did the 1 percent do it?

By that point, my thirst for increasing my Financial IQ was unquenchable. I had the good fortune of reading Robert Kiyosaki's *Rich Dad, Cash Flow Quadrant.* From that book, I learned how money works and that there were other ways than what I'd been originally taught to protect and multiply our wealth—better ways with less risk and greater upside. I realized I did *not* have to rely on the gyrations of the stock market for my family's future well-being.

WALL STREET'S NOT THE ANSWER

If you're reading this book, then you're probably in a similar position that I was—granted, you may not have triplets. But you are probably tired of the Wall Street casino, and tired of the advice your financial advisor is giving you. You've heard all the conventional wisdom out there that says, "put your money in a 401k," "pay off your house," "expect a 5 to 7 percent return on your investments," "dollar cost average," "diversify," and on and on. Now you're questioning if that's really the best you can do.

My answer is simple: no. You can do better. And that's what this book is all about: investing like the top 1 percent do by changing your mindset and developing a comprehensive wealth strategy to live life on your own terms. In this way, you'll have Freedom of Money, Purpose, Time, and Relationship, and create a legacy for your family. But there's a catch.

What I'm about to share with you isn't a set of steps that promise if you take one after the other, you'll be rich. I won't discuss whether you should invest in the stock market or how. I will discuss an alternative strategy that the wealthy have mastered since the Rockefellers and Rothschilds, one that often yields 40 percent returns and beyond. But before going there, it's important to step back and approach your wealth building from a holistic point of view, as the title suggests. Being wealthy is more than simply a matter of accumulating a portfolio of assets. It is a comprehensive expression of your mental, physical, *and* financial well-being.

THE ANSWER IS MULTIFACETED

If you're looking for a book to help you diversify your stock portfolio, this is not the book for you. I don't have any advice for anyone who is satisfied with conventional investing. And if that's you, great! There's no shortage of literature out there about how to stay in the stock market. Likewise, if you don't think you can or don't want to change your worldview, you won't get much out of what I have to tell you.

This is a book about expanding your Financial IQ and taking control of your wealth, which you will learn is antithetical to traditional investment strategies. This is a framework for building and following a holistic wealth strategy that will get you returns quick enough for you to actually take back control of your life.

In the first part, Setting Up Success, I'll tell you my story about how I came to develop this wealth strategy, why we don't feel we can manage our own money, and what's really preventing us from amassing the fortunes we'd like. Learning from my own experiences, and seeing the proof reflected in my clients, I know everyone needs to feel empowered to take control of their own finances. Most people I work with are smart, competent, industrious individuals. All of them have the capability to control their finances, but very few of them *think* that they can. They think they need a financial advisor to tell them what to do. After all, according to the traditional roadmap to success, as laid out by financial planners and companies interested in getting you to participate in their 401ks, only certain professionals should manage money, lest those funds are frittered away and wasted. While I do stress building a team of the right professionals to support you is important, I know that, if you're a hardworking professional who has earned enough money to invest in the stock market, then you have the intellectual and analytical tools to manage your own money.

Of course, having the ability sometimes isn't enough–you have to be able to work around what might be blocking you from achieving the wealth you desire. In Chapter 2, I'll cover the top three wealth disrupters, the biggest obstacles to building wealth (hint: Wall Street is one of them), and discuss how to move beyond them.

Then I'll follow that up with a discussion of what it means to be wealthy—truly, holistically wealthy. Having the kind of wealth that allows you The Four Freedoms™ of Purpose, Location, Money, and Relationships, a concept created by Dan Sullivan, co-founder of Strategic Coach®.

In the second part, Engineering a Holistic Wealth Strategy, I'll walk you through the five phases of my investment strategy: developing your mindset, expanding your learning, creating a wealth infrastructure, repositioning your assets, and building massive passive income.

Many of my clients want to skip over the mindset phase and go right to stock market alternatives, but I find that it is actually the most essential step toward experiencing financial freedom. Once you've adopted a growth mindset, you can finally begin acting on a holistic wealth strategy. You cannot grow your wealth and feel comfortable and confident investing in alternative strategies without changing your mindset.

All of us were brought up with certain limiting beliefs, whether that's having a scarcity mentality when you should have an abundance mentality or simply thinking that 7 percent growth is the absolute best you can get on your investments. Either way, to start living a truly wealthy life, you have to be curious to learn more about building wealth and eager to imagine a future for yourself beyond the scope of conventional wisdom. In fact, that's a prerequisite for developing a wealth-building mindset. If you cannot efficiently envision your financial future, you will not be able to take the steps needed to get there. So this book will start there, by developing a wealth-building mindset.

Once you've begun challenging the limiting beliefs that may be hindering you, in Phase 2, you will explore how to expand your learning. Here you'll discover how to increase your Financial IQ, which means learning as much as possible—in fact, you should never stop trying to learn more—about ways to build wealth. The highest-grossing and performing people in the world continually grow their Financial IQ. They're constantly reading new things and spending their time with similarly driven individuals. They're always trying to level up, to do more, and to go farther.

Whether or not you start hanging out with multimillionaires and reading six books a month, to achieve that all-around extraordinary life, you'll also need to expand your Mindset IQ and your Health IQ. As much as we might not like to hear it, a wealthy lifestyle has to include healthy mental and physical habits. At the time of his death, Steve Jobs was one of the world's wealthiest people in terms of his raw valuation, but ultimately, he wasn't able to access even a fraction of that wealth because he died before he could enjoy it. If you are spending all of your time working, barely seeing your family, eating poorly, and never exercising, all in the name of generating a few more hours of income, you will not be as wealthy—let alone as happy—as you could be if you developed a holistic attitude toward your wealth that includes a healthy lifestyle.

Once you've started the path of increasing your Financial, Mindset and Health IQs, you'll be equipped with the ability to invest in yourself and challenge any leftover internal biases, so you can start investing in your financial future. I discuss this in Phase 3, where I teach you how to build your wealth infrastructure. Here you'll learn about tax strategies to reduce your biggest expense and discover how to become your own bank through the infinite banking concept. You'll learn how to build a fortress around your wealth and family as well as how to create a dream team of professionals to support your personal and financial growth.

At this point, you'll be ready to take action. But where will you get the money to start investing in these alternative approaches? Phase 4 will help you do just that as you learn about asset repositioning. Here I talk about converting existing assets to cash-flowing, risk-adjusted, higher-performing, predictable, and tax-efficient assets. You'll also learn how to target IRAs and 401ks and to optimize your home equity. The final phase is all about expanding upon what you started in Phase 4. You can achieve massive financial expansion through a variety of specific strategies based on a multidimensional investment thesis. Get ready! Phase 5 is a fun chapter.

I end the book with a quick case study of myself employing the very same framework I discuss in this book. By following it, I've created successful habits that have improved much more than just my immediate investment portfolio. I truly am walking the talk and living the dream—yes, clichés, but they are true and appropriately describe what I do and how I live. Which might beg the question: who am I?

ALLOW ME TO INTRODUCE MYSELF

For a long time, I've known a couple of things about what I wanted out of life. I wanted to challenge myself and serve my country, so I became an officer in the Marine Corps. I wanted to start a business, now I've created three. I wanted to start a family and give them incredible opportunities, and I have: I am grateful for having four amazing children who have now grown and prospered. I wanted to learn Italian with my wife: now I'm fluent in it, with a house in Italy that I visit on tax-free flights (more on that later). I wanted to do an Ironman: now, I've completed one.

I'm proud of all of these accomplishments, but I mention them to illustrate a point: nowhere among these goals is being wealthy. All the same, each of them requires a certain amount of broad wealth to make them possible. It might seem obvious written out, but that notion has been absolutely foundational to both how I personally view money and the holistic wealth strategy at the heart of this book.

I grew up in a middle-class family. My parents were the first people, but not the last nor only, to teach me to follow the well-trod path to success: go to school, get good grades, land a good job in law, medicine, or corporate America, and set aside money in a 401k or IRA.

After graduating from a top-fifty university and serving my country in the Marines, I began climbing the corporate ladder. On the advice of a financial advisor, I invested 10 to 20 percent of my income into my company's 401k, expecting a 7 percent return. I was making money, doing well, and evidently on track to leading a good life.

With more income, my cost of living quickly ballooned. My tax rate increased, keeping up the house became more expensive, and the cost of raising our family skyrocketed. When we had our triplets, our expenses effectively quadrupled, and it became all the more important to accrue a sizable nest egg.

Going by the traditional roadmap to success I'd grown up with, things were going great. I was making more money than I ever had before and slowly gathering more wealth through careful investments. The only problem was that, despite hitting all the benchmarks of success, I could see that I was only just making enough to support my family's lifestyle. I found myself having to work more and hence, be stressed more as I perpetually tried to keep pace with a life I wasn't satisfied with. Worst of all, I realized I wasn't fully present with my loved ones—the people I was doing all this work for.

That's when I started thinking: if I'm doing everything "right," why does it feel like I'm just keeping my head above water? I began truly reflecting on what I wanted out of my life and thinking about those core goals I've always had; basically, I started questioning what I wanted all this hard work to lead to. What I discovered is that the amount of wealth I was actually building didn't feel nearly compensatory to the amount of time I spent earning it. Even more dismaying, it didn't feel like I would ever have enough time or money to reach my goals.

That's when I started searching for alternatives to Wall Street, 401ks, IRAs, and other instruments of traditional wealth management. I read Robert Kiyosaki's *Rich Dad Poor Dad,* and like a light bulb turning on, I realized that I hadn't really understood how money worked my entire life. That book, along with *Cashflow Quadrant,* showed me that I needed to completely reassess how I viewed wealth in order to start building it the way I knew I needed to.

According to the traditional roadmap to success, like the one my parents and society told me to follow, wealth is a means to an end. On it, it becomes all too easy to get into a lifestyle dedicated just to making money (and investing it into the stock market and/or 401ks), which too often precludes actually using that money to live well. Money is important, but it doesn't do anyone any good unless it's being used to improve the quality of their life or someone else's.

This notion—that money should be the oxygen to fuel an extraordinary life, not be what a life is for—is why I founded Pantheon Investments. I want to help others discover this alternative path of empowerment and freedom. We're a niche private equity firm that architects wealth strategies and provides opportunities to enable investors to get off the conventional-wisdom bandwagon to regain control and live the life they always desired. Basically, my team and I establish infinite banking policies and find alternative assets non-correlated to the stock market that provide immediate cash flow, are low-risk, have tax efficiency, and earn attractive returns to investors. We help them wean off the stock market roller coaster into something that will hit their wealth goals in less than half the time and create generational wealth. Our mission is to help investors achieve financial freedom through investing in alternative private assets such as real estate.

I would never have founded Pantheon were it not for my own dissatisfaction with the well-trod path to success. I was on it long enough—far too long, actually—that I know the particular frustrations it can lead to. I have years of experience advising my clients on how to veer away from typical investments and into a position of controlling their wealth. Because I've been on this journey myself, I know how difficult it can be to get it started. But I assure you that once you reconceptualize how you want your money to work for you and start actively building your wealth, you'll be exponentially closer to the life you want to live.

NOW IT'S YOUR TURN

When I'm advising my clients, I always make sure that they understand that I have walked in their shoes. I didn't establish Pantheon Investments or even write this book as a thought experiment; everything I lay out here is cultivated from my own experience and dissatisfaction with the traditional road-map to success. In my story, there wasn't one existential crisis that led to my discoveries about wealth; instead, it was a series of frustrations and disappointments that progressively forced me to find an alternative. My goal is always to get my clients off that unhelpful path well before they have their own crises.

Although I've spent twenty years of my life creating a system of how to build wealth, first for myself and my family, and then for my clients, when I talk to people about how I made this money, more than 50 percent of them don't get it, primarily because they don't want to. They might be doctors, lawyers, or other business professionals. They think they're the smartest people in the room, that they know everything. And if they're the smartest people in the room, and they've been making traditional investments, then surely that must be the smartest thing for them to have done with their money, right?

I know that what I suggest you do isn't always easy, and some-times it might feel counterintuitive, but I assure you that if it works for my clients, me, and the top 1 percent, it can work for you too. You have the ambition to create real wealth and a general understanding of what the passive investing thesis looks like, but maybe you aren't sure how to get away from the stock market in a way that provides your family with the security it needs. Let me show you how it works for me.

PART 1

SETTING UP SUCCESS

Chapter 1

TAKING BACK CONTROL

Seeing your money drop overnight is painful. At the time of this writing in Q2 of 2022, the market is down by over 20 percent year to date. When I was invested in Wall Street, I was told repeatedly that my money was doing exactly what it was supposed to, that the market volatility was normal, but if I stayed the course, it would end up in positive territory. After meetings with my financial advisors, I'd walk away with this nagging feeling that I wasn't being shown the full picture, and that if I just had a bit more knowledge, I could grow my money well beyond the conservative projections I was given. It seemed that they were the only ones making money playing this game.

Once I questioned the meager returns my family was earning in our investment accounts, I cycled through financial advisors looking for different answers. Each of them gave me the same advice to stay in the stock market and be satisfied with my 7 percent returns. With the cost of living and college constantly rising, it takes nearly a million dollars to raise one kid today—and I've got four of them. Going by their advice, I wouldn't be able to retire comfortably nor give my family the lifestyle they deserved.

That's when I began this obsessive quest to learn how the 1 percent were generating wealth so I could do the same for myself and my family. I knew that if I didn't follow this passion, I'd regret it for the rest of my life. That quest has led me to an abundant lifestyle, to founding my own investment firm, to providing my family with the comfort and security I've always wanted to give them, and to creating a bigger impact by helping others achieve their wealth vision.

I know the pain you're feeling right now, the itching sensation that you could be doing so much better. I want to show you how I took that same feeling and spun it into the life that I have now.

There are four steps I took to really get back control of my money. First, I increased my Financial IQ by poring through thousands of hours of books, podcasts, and other resources. The discoveries I made based on that education helped me create the foundation of the holistic wealth strategy. With a proper understanding of how money actually works and the paradigm shift I needed to make, I became an Investor and invested in real estate and alternative assets. Finally, I became a Business Owner and founded my own business, both as a means to gain further financial independence and to be best positioned for taking advantage of tax incentives.

Before diving into how I built my wealth, it's important to understand how I view money in a general sense. I'm called to a Henry David Thoreau quote: "Wealth is the ability to fully experience life." That is, wealth is not an arbitrary number or a certain lifestyle. Money is like oxygen. We need it to live, but that doesn't mean we need to live for it.

I've spent much of my life building wealth, but I've never given myself a precise number I needed to reach in order to be "successful." Instead, I've constantly asked myself if the amount I have is enough to allow me and my family to fully experience life the way we want to. After many years of research and hard work, I am proud to say that I've built my wealth to a point where my family and I can experience the best things life has to offer. Our passive income, in fact, exceeds our lifestyle expenses, and I do not need to work to live. Now it's all about creating greater wealth to have a bigger impact on those we serve.

CONTROLLING MY TAXES

As my first business became more successful I got really tired of not knowing what our tax liability would be every year and having to unexpectedly pay significant amounts. Because I learned that it was possible to have a tax rate of zero as a business owner and investor, I continued searching for the right CPA firm that had this philosophy. My most insightful discovery was learning from Tom Wheelwright in his best-selling book, *Tax-Free Wealth*, that taxes should be viewed in an entirely different manner. The tax code isn't really a fine meant to be paid but rather is a series of incentives for business owners and investors. This is how the top 1 percent of wealth-builders had mastered their taxes, by partnering with the government to reduce their taxes legally. I was doggedly persistent in searching for the right CPA and finally found them after firing five different firms over several years. It took me a long time, huge frustrations, and high tax bills to get here, but the investment in the right firm paid off ten times over.

Most people, I learned, do not understand the tax code, and that includes many CPAs. That's reasonable considering that the thing is 6,000 pages long. Those who actually read it hardly get past the first page, which tells you that you legally have to pay taxes and not much else. The other 5,999 or so pages are mostly dedicated to incentivizing certain kinds of financial behavior for business owners and investors. *That*, both literally and metaphorically, is where the money is.

Incentives are the key to our tax code: it is designed to encourage people through incentives to start and maintain businesses and invest in things like real estate. We see that reflected in our nation's wealthiest individuals. Essentially all of them are entrepreneurs, savvy investors, or both. The ones who inherited their wealth inherited it from people in those categories.

Early in my quest to build wealth, I realized that I needed to get off of receiving income as a W-2 employee. If you're an employee, even a well-compensated one, you will always be at the mercy of the tax code. Think about it: the government incentivized somebody to create and run the company to give you a job, a job where your income will be taxed. We'll explore ways that you can take advantage of tax strategies later in the book, but generally speaking, the best move you can make is to stop paying taxes as an individual employee and start paying them as a business.

CONTROLLING MY FINANCIAL PLAN

Despite this great insight (that I needed to become a business owner instead of an employee), none of the three financial advisors I hired brought that up to me. Neither did the first four of my five CPA firms. I didn't go to business school, nor do I have any special mind for numbers or accounting, but the more I learned about the habits of the wealthy, the more I began to wonder why I wasn't being advised to follow those same habits. But upon further reflection and a little more research, I realized I wasn't the only one who missed out on the advice.

No one, not even financial advisors, is taught how to manage their money properly. It's comforting to assume that the people with the most academic accreditations are the most knowledgeable about growing wealth, but it's not actually the case. Financial planners went to school expressly to learn how to work with money, yet few of them are actually wealthy themselves. So I began to ask: if these are people advising others on how to grow wealth, why then are they not the wealthiest individuals?

The first answer is that school won't teach you how to be wealthy, even if you go there to learn how to work with money. When you go to college or graduate school, you're taught how to develop a skill that you can leverage into getting yourself a job; in essence, you're taught to work. This is especially true in business, law, or medical school, but it applies to liberal arts colleges and really any other kind of education. At school, you're taught how to make money, but nowhere are you taught how to protect and grow wealth.

It might seem counterintuitive, but the best way to make money is not only how to make it but also how to grow it. Even a casual observer can tell you that the wealthiest people don't only *make* their money—they *grow* it. Take Elon Musk for example, one of the wealthiest people on the planet. No one is signing a paycheck with his name on it to the tune of a couple hundred billion dollars; rather, his money is coming from a series of highly profitable businesses, acquisitions, and investments. All that wealth accrues mostly on its own because it has been exceedingly well managed through a strategy.

Meanwhile, traditional income from a paycheck is subject to the highest tax rate, and thus always exposed to an extreme amount of loss. For those wanting to retire or those who can no longer work, a traditional income also has a definite end date that is never guaranteed. Despite being the primary way most Americans make their living, working for a wage, no matter how large, is an extremely fragile source of income.

Yet for some reason, the American education system doesn't teach anyone how to steward their money. We are expected to rely on financial planners who end up going to school for years to learn how to advise others on how to manage their money, but nobody teaches them how to grow wealth—not yours or even their own. This is how you end up with a fleet of financial experts who don't know how to make themselves wealthy—let alone you. They rely on making their money off of fees from your hard-earned efforts.

As such, they are not incentivized to give good advice. Through my years of reading hundreds of books on the wealthy, as well as doing my own research, I discovered that the real truth about financial advisors is that, more than anything else, they are salespeople. They make their money through assets under management so their interest is not mutually aligned with you, it is focused on increasing their fees through the products they can offer in the stock market. Further, they continue to collect their fees whether the market is up or down. There are hundreds of alternative investment options—many of which, you will learn, are significantly lower risk and more lucrative than traditional options—that financial planners will never tell you about, simply because they don't have any monetary stake in them. When investing in direct private investments, investors can enjoy performance-based investments that are mutually aligned with both general partners and investors.

This shocks people when I tell them: financial planners have a fiduciary responsibility to grow your portfolio, but that really only extends as far as the stock market is concerned. These people aren't necessarily malicious; rather, they have only so many kinds of financial products they can sell you. Even if you have an investment opportunity that will grow your wealth, because of the nature of their business, your financial advisors might be incentivized to suggest against it. You need to ensure that the people surrounding your wealth actually want to see it grow.

This is why you have to start taking control of your own money. Later in the book, I'll teach you how to build a team of individuals to support your holistic wealth strategy, but you have to always be at the center of it. Hire as many financial advisors as you like—they will always be selling their particular line before they actually help you grow your wealth. Always remember there is no one more invested in your own money than you, and you owe it to yourself to learn how to cultivate it. Since you're reading this book, you're already well on your way there.

CONTROLLING MY INVESTMENTS

Once I was thoroughly disillusioned with financial planners, I began searching for my own investments. While my children were still young and we were living in Denver, my wife and I started looking for local real estate we could buy. I remember driving around suburban Denver, my wife bribing our four kids with lollipops in the back of the car to keep them quiet, while we visited potential investment properties. It turns out that visiting investment properties with four rambunctious, wailing children wasn't conducive to making big investment decisions.

The more I learned about actively investing in real estate, the more I felt the risk was too great. Wherever I looked, I could never find cash-flowing properties that made the numbers work, and I didn't have the capacity or the interest in being a hands-on landlord. I also knew that I was competing against full-time active rental property investors who knew the market inside and out. At the time, I worked for a tech consultancy business while raising a big family; I didn't even have time to fix the toilets in my own house.

Rental real estate investments are a natural first step for people trying to leave the stock market, but they're not always the best place for your money. Active real estate investing is a competitive field, and there are many people for whom it's a full-time job. These people understand the comps (the values of comparable properties), they understand all the nuances of the rental market, and they have years of experience in that realm. Unless you're truly serious about making managing individual properties your full-time job, small-scale real estate investment does not scale and won't be the best way for you to build wealth.

When I came to this realization myself, I felt frustrated and lost. I knew that I had a decent amount of money to invest, and I knew that I didn't want it in the stock market or a 401k, but I didn't quite know where to put it if not in traditional rental real estate. That's how I discovered passive investing in real estate syndications.

Real estate syndications are groups of investors who, under the banner of one or several management companies, collectively invest in a large property like an apartment building. In this use, passive investment refers to any investment that you need to spend very little time managing. Here's how it works.

Let's compare a $250,000 investment in a real estate syndication versus one in a standard, single-family rental property. On the surface, you might think the single-family home is the better option, as you get to own all of it. But what happens when you can't find a renter? Or the renter you do have is behind on their payments? Or the roof needs to be replaced? In any of those instances and many others, your rental income drops to $0. Not only that, you have to keep up with your tenant or hire a property manager—both of which can be massive drains on your time or money.

Compare that to an investment in multifamily real estate syndication. In one such syndication, you're one of a number of limited partners on a deal. You'll get access to a completely top-notch, quality asset, like a $50 million, 300-unit apartment building in a rapidly growing area. You'll be investing alongside a professional team with systems in place to ensure that rent is collected on time, facilities are managed, tenants are satisfied, and forced appreciation is driven to increase the value of the property. Through the experience and market focus of the syndicator, you'll also get access to off-market properties and some of the strongest markets in the country. You won't need to live geographically close to the property, nor will you be limited to the whims of your local housing market. Best of all, you won't have to spend any of your precious time managing the property. You just write the check and start receiving your passive income.

There are other passive investments you can make, such as oil and gas, self-storage, mobile home parks, hotels, car washes, agriculture, and so on. After twenty years of research and investment, I have found that on a risk-adjusted basis multifamily real estate syndications are the crown jewel of investing. They are non-correlated to the stock market, have strong tax advantages, provide predictable passive income, and have lucrative potential upon exit through forced appreciation. However, no financial planner will tell you about them; in fact, if you ask, they'll probably downplay their profitability and say they are risky. This is because the planner has nothing to gain from you taking your money out of the stock market and putting it in this kind of investment. Think: is it riskier to have your capital in the markets subject to global, political, and other swings that you have no control of, or in a tangible asset of housing, which is one of the base human elements in Maslow's hierarchy of needs? Only through diverging from the traditional roadmap to success was I able to discover this gold mine of passive income.

CONTROLLING MY BUSINESS

As I started to make alternative investments and see the results from them, I began sharing with others what I was learning and how well it was paying off. At the time, I was running a tech consulting firm that I'd created, but there was something missing from it. I wasn't completely satisfied with it.

Through Dan Sullivan's Strategic Coach® Program, I learned about a powerful concept called Unique Ability®, which centers on doubling down on your strengths and where you create the most value for others. This focuses on your conative abilities or instinctual wiring where things come easily and naturally for you. By focusing your energy on the highest value activities and building a team around you to do everything else, you can exponentially grow your business and be fulfilled doing it. I enjoyed the tech company, but at times it could feel like a job. Entrepreneurs often start their first business based on their current expertise, market, and relationships. A huge insight I discovered in Strategic Coach is that we should be focused on building a business that aligns to our unique ability and captures our biggest opportunity. I'm most passionate about building trusting and meaningful relationships with people. I like solving their problems and adding value to their lives. That's a huge part of why I wrote this book. My consulting business was one way I could express that, but it certainly wasn't the only way. I wanted to create more impact and be more passionate about my energies.

When I started asking myself what was the biggest opportunity I had, I immediately came back to my obsession with building wealth. I had been toying around with the idea of developing software to help people build their wealth with this alternative strategy, but I found myself more interested in working directly with clients to help them grow their wealth than the software business model. From my own experience with alternative investments, I knew there was a wide-open market for helping people get away from Wall Street. So I made a role for myself, partnered with best-in-class syndicators I had known for years, invested my own money, and focused on the investor relations side of private equity investing. Only well after I founded Pantheon did I realize there was an entire industry of capital raisers and alternative investment firms.

Many businesses like ours develop out of more traditional approaches to private equity, but Pantheon is different. We knew we wanted to help people achieve financial freedom in less than half the time they thought they could and to educate them about the alternative strategy of the top 1 percent to do so. Instead of trying to shoehorn our business model into an existing structure, we let this core focus and our values be at the heart of what we stand for. We don't focus on what the competition is doing, but rather on always delivering maximum value to our clients. Our business model now includes the infinite banking solution, which has long been a foundational strategy to Family Offices and the ultra-wealthy for years. Here we can assist clients to build a capital warehouse for their wealth that compounds tax-free, is passed on to heirs tax-free, creates a tax-free income stream, and can be leveraged to acquire other assets as you become your own bank. We continue to provide solutions and educate clients on how they can protect and multiply their wealth.

Once we got Pantheon off the ground, I found myself exponentially closer to living a life of Freedom of Purpose, Freedom of Money, Freedom of Time, and Freedom of Relationship. Yes, this can be directly attributed to implementing the holistic wealth strategy I am about to share with you. I believe our journey in life as entrepreneurs should be holistic in nature to achieve not only Freedom of Money, but also Freedom of Purpose to do what you love to do, Freedom of Time to do it when you want, and Freedom of Relationship to work with who you want to work with. I love working with entrepreneurs because they are big thinkers, inquisitive, and make things happen. Before achieving these freedoms I worried about having financial security for my family and my business and wanted to have more passion and impact for the work I was doing, but now I am on a strong trajectory that creates a future that is always bigger than my past. This has become my life's work—I don't want to stop doing it until I literally have to. Pantheon has given me purpose, drive, and tangible examples of people I've directly helped make massive changes in their wealth. I couldn't ask for more.

I think this illustrates the other key facet of my journey to financial freedom. Getting off a W-2 and moving away from Wall Street are great steps toward building your wealth, but they don't mean anything if those financial decisions aren't enabling you to lead a happier, fuller life. For me, to lead that kind of life, I had to make a business for myself that empowered me to do the work I wanted to do.

> Financial freedom means more than making a bunch of money: it means actually having the time and agency to do what you want. It means having room to breathe.

IT'S TIME FOR YOU TO TAKE CONTROL

Understanding how to make your taxes work for you, letting go of traditional financial planning advice, investing in alternative assets, founding your own business—any of these actions might be right for you. The philosophy central to all of them, however, is taking back control of your money and thus your life.

If you've been working with a traditional financial planner up until now, you've been trusting an uninvested party with quite literally the bulk of your personal value. On the well-trod path to success, this is a sensible thing to do. But what other foundational aspects of your life do you hand over to someone who may not have your best interest at heart? According to that traditional roadmap, it's also sensible to give away most of your money to taxes and to play it safe in the stock market. The financial model most of us have been taught simply doesn't make sense. You're not crazy for being dissatisfied with it.

If I could give my past self—still bogged down in 401ks and 529s—one piece of advice, it would be what I'm telling you now: learn how money works and take back control of your wealth. That is the most important thing that I have done to achieve my life goals. And it will be for you too.

Now that you have a sense of how my journey went, you can begin to imagine what yours will look like. But as with any journey, it's vital to know what risks you're heading into. In our financial system, there are three major wealth destroyers that can jeopardize your money and security. Once you have a sense of what you need to look out for, you can chart a course for your success that nimbly avoids these pitfalls. Let's explore them now.

Chapter 2

THE THREE WEALTH DISRUPTERS

THE RISKS OF A "SAFE BET"

My father-in-law was a very generous man. Throughout his life, he gave my wife a lot, including many gifts of stock. His thinking, the conventional thinking, was that this was a more lucrative, safer way to share his wealth with his family than by simply giving out lump sums of cash. One of the main stocks he gave my wife was Kodak; at the time it was one of the most stable stock options. It was considered a total blue chip company, to be so secure, in fact, that many companies invested pension funds into it.

I probably don't need to tell you what happened next, but in case I do—the company went bankrupt in 2012 and the stock crashed. Almost overnight, my father-in-law's years of generosity evaporated in the stock market. As much as it was a financial loss for my wife, it stung beyond that: she felt, rightly, that her father had been cheated.

MANKOFF

"On Wall Street today, news of lower interest rates sent the stock market up, but then the expectation that these rates would be inflationary sent the market down, until the realization that lower rates might stimulate the sluggish economy pushed the market up, before it ultimately went down on fears that an overheated economy would lead to a reimposition of higher interest rates."

The scenario above is why the stock market is one of the three biggest wealth destroyers out there. We've all been told, "Well, the stock market is still the safest option, and over time, it corrects itself." But how many people do you know who, like my wife, have lost an unimaginable amount of wealth riding on the "safe bet" of the stock market? Even if it weren't so misleading, there are other investments to be made that can readily make you over twice as much as traditional investing. Viewed from that perspective, you can see how Wall Street and the dozens of mechanisms in place to feed it aren't "safe bets" at all—they're pitfalls.

It's not just the stock market that's eating your nest egg. The other two largest wealth disrupters stem from the government: taxes and government-sponsored qualified plans. Most people take investing in a 401k and paying ludicrously large portions of their wealth in taxes as givens, as inefficient as they might seem, because we are assured there really isn't anything else you should do, in the case of 401ks, or that you can do, in the case of taxes.

If I could sum up the thesis statement of this book in one sentence, it would be this: there *is* something you can do about it and that begins with understanding what's standing in your way, what systems are out there ready to gobble up your hard-earned money. Before you can develop an alternative to the traditional wealth portfolio, you have to know what you're going up against. That's what this chapter is all about.

THE THREE WEALTH DISRUPTERS
WEALTH DISRUPTER #1: TAXES

Every time spring comes around, we are all reminded of the financial devastation of taxes. Whether you think of them as a tool for wealth redistribution or civic planning, there is no getting around the fact that taxes are the primary way that middle-class people are kept from the upper echelons of wealth. Unfortunately, most people accept the ridiculous statements their CPAs hand them as a given and just try to do their best to plan for the worst. But it doesn't have to be this way. One of the few differences between truly wealthy Americans and the majority of others is that the upper 1 percent knows precisely how much they have to pay in taxes well before April 15th, and most importantly, they know how to minimize those payments.

I'm not going to get into politics in this book, but I will tell you that if you are serious about generating holistic wealth, you have to learn how to leverage the existing tax code to protect your money. There is simply no other way to turn your hard work into a truly wealthy lifestyle for you and your family. Do you really want to work for four to six months out of the year just to pay your taxes?

Well before I was running businesses and dealing with the headaches of their taxes, every year I became incensed at the amount of money my CPAs told me I'd have to pay in taxes. Right around March 30th (or later, in the cases of the particularly disorganized firms I've worked with), I'd be informed that I owed a large six-figure amount to the government. I was told this quite casually, as if it wouldn't completely rearrange my finances. That was bad enough on its own, but the part that I couldn't bear was the fact that I was totally unprepared for such a large amount. Receiving these estimates just two weeks out from having to pay them boggled my mind. But I kept on working within the tax structures I knew because I couldn't find an alternative out there.

In the beginning days of founding my businesses, I wasn't paying very much in taxes because my companies were young and had little income to be taxed. But as my companies grew, I saw how we were being walloped by aggressive taxation. Both my businesses were working with large, Fortune 500 companies at the time, and our revenue kept expanding so I was able to employ more prestigious CPA firms. They didn't make a difference; the only things the larger firms got me were bigger fees. Reading the tax code and researching it, I learned that it's just a roadmap of incentives for business owners and investors, so I didn't understand why these supposed experts couldn't identify any substantial tax savings.

Over the past twenty years of learning about how money works, I've hired five CPA firms and, as I mentioned earlier, I fired four of them. Many accountants seem to view their jobs as passing the buck down to their clients and maybe half-heartedly explaining why it is that they have to pay so much. Most CPAs are too cautious, too afraid to aggressively use the tax code. And why wouldn't they be? As long as their clients can afford their retainers, CPAs have very little incentive to try ambitious strategies to maximize their client's wealth; instead, they'll play it safe, even if it costs the client thousands of dollars. I knew this wouldn't work for me and my desire to get to a tax rate of zero, so I started to look doggedly for a CPA who would proactively create a strategic tax plan to legally reduce my taxes. I implore you to do the same.

If you're a W-2 employee making a solid income and have under a few million dollars in net worth, you will probably encounter a standard slate of financial advice about taxes. If you are comfortable with getting the same advice the other 95 percent are, you won't be able to mitigate this top wealth disrupter. But if you have a desire to build true generational wealth, you have to get a different type of advice.

Later in the book, I'll detail some of the things I looked for in a firm, but the best thing I can tell you about how to find the right team is that you have to be persistent. Learning about money is hard, both because it's complicated and because there are institutions that make it an intentionally obtuse process. In my journey toward building wealth, I stumbled into many pitfalls and had many sleepless nights worrying about what I would do and if I could do it. Since you're reading this book, hopefully, you'll have less of those on your own journey, but even if you do have a few missteps, you have to keep going. Without that same burning persistence, you won't have the courage and drive to fire your mediocre CPA or to spend the hours of research needed to find the right one.

> If you would like a list of our preferred CPA firms that support this strategy, sign up to be a member of our Investor Community here: https://pantheoninvest.com/investor-signup/.

After a long time, I finally found a firm that actually knew how to navigate the tax code. Incidentally, I went with the same firm that advised Robert Kiyosaki, my favorite financial researcher. I've been with them for seven years now, and I can tell you that my personal marginal effective rate last year was 14 percent and my goal is to get to zero. I've done deep research on taxes in my life, but I credit them and their incredible knowledge for getting me such a low rate. Much of this book is about taking back control of your money, but I cannot overstate how unbelievably valuable it is to have the right people helping you make financial decisions. Taking control doesn't mean going it alone.

Once I found that CPA firm, we started by building a strategic tax plan, which included a unique entity structure for my businesses that takes advantage of the tax incentives available, minimizing the amount I have to pay. Since everyone's personal financial situations are different—especially in a country where tax codes can vary so much from state to state—a bespoke approach to your taxes is the only way you're going to really get around them. (My tax return last year was over 200 pages.) There are a few tricks that I have learned along the way—one is you must be an active partner in implementing your tax plan; however, almost anyone who runs a business can utilize it to make their money work for them.

I'm serious. You can purchase a vacation house and get a tax deduction—if you rent it out for fourteen days or more a year. Let's say you have a few client development parties or retreats at that house, events you can even invite your friends and family to participate in. If you do that, your house becomes a kind of venue space for your business, making your payments to maintain it suddenly deductible.

Another savvy tax strategy you could make is to give your adult, in-school child a place—and a job. If you're paying for your kid to live off-campus while they're at college, you can divert some of your income to hire them as a part-time employee and set up the housing as a rental property. Since you're now providing housing through your real estate rental and hiring your child, you can deduct all of the expenses of the property as well as the wages you are paying, too.

The above are just a couple of ways my CPAs and I work with the tax code, but there are dozens, if not hundreds more ways to do it. They just require some creativity and a team of financial allies who are just as excited as you are about building real wealth.

In order to take advantage of these opportunities, however, you have to be a business owner or investor. A business owner should be targeting to pay 20 percent in taxes while an investor can be targeting zero. If you're just getting a W-2, you can't really make these kinds of moves. If you're not currently a business owner, become one with a side hustle, as I'll talk about later, and if you are, seriously reconsider how you structure your tax plan. That's how you're going to make the most (or the least) of your taxes.

WEALTH DISRUPTER #2: THE STOCK MARKET

No matter what company they work for, every financial planner will tell you the same thing: the market will go up, the market will go down, but you'll make a 7 percent rate of return over the long haul. Considering that this money is almost passively generated, that sounds pretty good, but it actually obfuscates the way Wall Street locks people's wealth away from real growth.

Say you have $4 million invested in the stock market at retirement. The exact numbers will change, but financial planners will then simulate your projected lifespan to determine how much money you can withdraw in retirement. On average they estimate earning 7 percent of your wealth every year, and then you can withdraw about 4 percent of your money out of the market to live on at retirement age, netting you roughly $160,000 a year. From that number, you'll have to pay your taxes, and if I'm certain on one thing, it's that taxes will be rising in the future. After paying your taxes and fees to your financial planner over all of those years, your net spendable income may be closer to $100,000.

I'm certain an income of a hundred grand is not even close to what you thought you would be living on with a nest egg of $4 million and, if you're anything like me, that's far from enough to live the kind of lifestyle your hard work should have gotten you. If you have built up a $4 million portfolio, that means you've probably worked most of your adult life building a remarkable amount of wealth. That's money coming from business ventures, years at the office, careful budgeting, and probably a few sacrifices in your personal life. If you've spent all that time making so much money, why, then, would you spend the last years of your life living as if you hadn't worked nearly that hard?

When I explain it like this and dispel traditional planning myths like deferring taxes and building a lump sum portfolio for retirement, my clients tend to appreciate my argument, but it's hard for them to see that 7 percent figure as what it truly is. Think about it this way: my wife has a little bit of money still invested in the stock market. At this point, it's mostly sentimental for her, but I digress. Investors tend to lose sight of the fact that in a given year their investments might be up 17 percent. The year after that, even 20 percent, and the next year 21 percent. At the time of this writing in 2022, however, the S&P is down over 13 percent. You average enough years like this together, and you end up at about that 7 percent figure—that's held true for as long as Wall Street has existed. But when the market goes down 13 percent, you're losing 13 percent of *all* that money you invested; you're actually losing *more* money than you would have had you invested *less* in the stock market. This makes it in effect exponentially harder to recoup your losses, trapping you in a cycle of riding the stock market without any sign of an off-ramp.

That's what the stock market will do to you: it'll make you

feel like you can never safely leave once you're in it. That's by design. The stock market, safe bet or not (and I'm telling you—it isn't one), is not designed to make you or me wealthy. It's a rigged game and is designed to make a certain class of people, a certain circle of individuals highly invested in it and its adjacent industries, a huge amount of wealth at the expense of diligent, accomplished, mostly middle-class Americans. If you read this book and want to stay in the stock market, that's fine, but in writing it, I want to make sure that every person who continues to invest in this wealth-destroying system knows precisely what it is that they have gotten themselves into. Stay or go, the choice is yours, but know that you can do so much better.

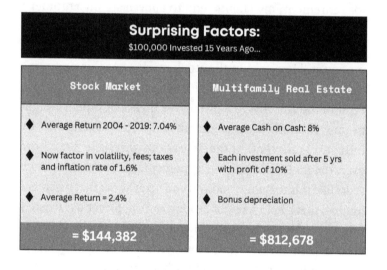

Surprising Factors:
$100,000 Invested 15 Years Ago...

Stock Market	Multifamily Real Estate
◆ Average Return 2004 - 2019: 7.04%	◆ Average Cash on Cash: 8%
◆ Now factor in volatility, fees; taxes and inflation rate of 1.6%	◆ Each investment sold after 5 yrs with profit of 10%
◆ Average Return = 2.4%	◆ Bonus depreciation
= $144,382	= $812,678

WEALTH DISRUPTER #3: GOVERNMENT-QUALIFIED PLANS

Of all three wealth disrupters, government-qualified plans are the most pernicious. They may not cost you or your family quite as much money as the other disrupters, but they promise so much more and deliver so much less. Even people content on the well-trod path to success have their suspicions about the stock market, and they certainly know the pain of tax season, but almost no one appreciates how threatening to wealth government-sponsored qualified plans really are. These are the golden handcuffs of the government, ensnaring millions of Americans with promises of tax-deferred wealth and stability.

These plans lure investors by saying, essentially, that backers can avoid paying taxes on the contributions they make to them now and defer them into the future. On paper, this has some obvious benefits; namely, by the time you're paying taxes on these sums of money, you will have much more of it appreciated. This is how every financial planner, employer, and government institution sells 401ks, IRAs, 529s, and the like.

I can't predict the future, but let me ask you: ten, twenty, or twenty-five years from now, do you think taxes are going to be higher or lower? The adage "death and taxes" comes to mind. What this means is that the money you are paying in taxes now, assuming you continue to be profitable in your business and investments, is the lowest it will ever be. Therefore, deferring your tax payments into the future means you will be paying a much higher tax rate on your income than when you made those payments in the first place. Making matters worse, when you retire and start withdrawing that money (usually about 4 percent or even less of it a year), you are actually taxed at the highest tax rate of ordinary income. The money is technically "yours," but you have to pay huge amounts in taxes on it, significantly more than if you had just paid the taxes upfront. Wouldn't you rather pay taxes on the seed than the harvest?

And that's before you account for the ways you can manage your own money and avoid the worst of tax season. Once you factor in some of the tax strategies I've discussed and will explain further in the book, you'll realize that there are even more ways to pay even less on your income. You won't be able to do any of that if you're stuck in a 401k or an IRA; instead, you'll be at the mercy of the rigidity of a government-qualified plan.

Here's what I did to break out of my 401k. After doing my research, I bit the bullet, paid the 10 percent withdrawal penalty and the taxes, and left my 401k behind. As soon as I could, I took that money to a multifamily real estate syndication. I estimated that it would take me about five or six years to break even in that investment opportunity, but in reality, I was able to break even in only three and a half years and offset all of the taxes through my tax strategy. I've never looked back. That money is obviously subject to long-term capital gains, but because of something called bonus depreciation, I'm able to vastly lower the amount I'm taxed on, and, strategically, if I stay in the right asset class I can defer taxes until my death *and* get a stepped-up basis on those assets when passing them to my heirs. Because I've invested that money into a real estate syndication, I'm able to take advantage of what's called a cost segregation study. This study analyzes all the features of a building that wear out with use, such as the HVAC, the carpeting, the lights in the building, and so on. Once a cost segregation specialist has assigned a value to that, we can then bring that depreciation forward into the first few years of operation. If my initial investment was $100,000, I can potentially receive up to 80 percent of that in bonus depreciation to offset passive income and gains.

THE BOTTOM LINE: GET PAST THE THREE WEALTH DISRUPTERS

The above types of strategies are what the ultra-wealthy have been using for years, and you can bet this kind of maneuvering would be completely impossible for them if their money was tucked away in a government-sponsored qualified plan. Neither would it work if they outsourced it all to a wealth planner and rode it out on the whims of the stock market or lost 20 to 35 percent of it every year to taxes.

When I advocate for taking back control of your money, I don't just write that as a platitude—having total control over your wealth is literally the only way you can grow it. As you continue your own journey toward holistic wealth, you need to be clear-eyed about the wealth disrupters that stand in your way; it's no coincidence that all three disrupters place barriers between you and your money. If you can see taxes, the stock market, and government-qualified plans for what they really are, you can avoid them and get yourself and your family on the path to real wealth.

* * *

When I tell my clients about these wealth disrupters, I think back to the gift of stock my father-in-law gave to his daughter. He didn't have to do that, but he wanted to provide her and her family with what, to him, seemed like a stable source of income. Unfortunately, he'd been misled, as many people have been, into thinking that the traditional roadmap to success was the right one.

The majority of his generosity vanished in the stock market, not because of his mismanagement or lack of skills, but because he didn't understand that these systems that have been touted as the pillars of financial stability are in fact quite shaky. Our family was able to withstand the losses that my father-in-law's gifts suffered, but many can't. I don't want you or anyone else to lose the value of their hard work by giving up control to one or any of these wealth disrupters.

Now that we've seen what's blocking you from real wealth, it's time to explore what wealth really is and what it provides. I'll introduce you to the core psychology of money that many of us fall prey to, and I'll share with you a better way to conceptualize it. I'll also unpack The Four Freedoms™ that wealth provides and how to draft a vision statement that builds off your relationship to them. With that foundation in place, you'll begin practicing the kind of deep thinking and free dreaming necessary to achieve real wealth.

Chapter 3

BECOMING FREE

THINKING DEEPLY AND DREAMING FREELY ABOUT YOUR GOALS

Most Americans spend more time planning their summer vacation than they do their financial future. I'll admit, going to Italy can be much more fun than reading about taxes. However, being disconnected from their wealth leads people to feel financially stagnated and unable to lead the lives they truly want (or even go on the amazing summer vacations they dream of and not Italy, again). Financial planning can seem daunting, like it's something only the over-educated or highly-invested can do, but I'm here to tell you that it's not that hard at all. It requires a little research and patience, sure, but before all that, you just need to think deeply and dream freely about what you want your money to do for you. If you're able to plan a family vacation, then you have the forethinking necessary to plan your financial future. And that planning begins with some questions.

WHAT DO YOU REALLY WANT YOUR LIFE TO BE LIKE?

Almost everyone says they want to have more money, but what they really mean is that they want more freedom—money is just the most direct way to achieve it. Wealth alone won't get you there, however; you need to have total control of that wealth in order to actually experience true freedom.

Taken at face value, The Four Freedoms™ are obvious components of a wealthy lifestyle, but you have to articulate them for *yourself* to understand what it is that *you* want to achieve. In this chapter, I'll take you through the process of creating a vision statement for yourself that builds on these freedoms. Through its creation, you may discover that one freedom is more important to you than another; in fact, I'd be surprised if each one matters to you in the same way. Achieving clarity on what doors your wealth will open in this way, through this self-examination, is the final step you need to take before making the tangible moves toward building your wealth.

THE PSYCHOLOGY OF MONEY

First we must unpack the psychology of money. We typically think of money as a goal. Financial planners often advise their clients to set benchmarks for the amount of growth they want to see, and employers usually bring people on by first asking them how much they want to make in a year. This conceptualization of money—as a means unto itself—gets many of us in trouble. When someone wins the lottery, for instance, they tend to become miserable within a few years because their goals are limited to just getting all that money; once they have it, they run out of the drive, out of the essential excitement of life. Conversely, look at billionaires like Richard Branson and Bill Gates, who have spent so much of their lives and their vast fortunes on philanthropic endeavors. Obviously, these two individuals have thought very seriously about what it is they want to do with their money, and the result is that our planet gets to benefit from the dozens, if not hundreds, of charitable projects they steward.

Our brains are hardwired to perceive money as something that has inherent value. Of course, the whole idea of currency is that it doesn't have innate value, but it's difficult to keep sight of this as you grow your bank accounts. When I work with my clients, one of the first things I do with them is help them realign their mindset. If you can't change how you think about money, you probably won't be able to change how much of it you have.

Oftentimes I'll be talking with my wife about our investments, and we'll get totally lost in what we are discussing. We'll be worrying about one thing or excited about another, trying to piece together what our next opportunity will be without really thinking about why we're doing that work. Looking at our spreadsheets and tracking documents—at too many numbers to keep in our heads—it becomes necessary to step back and ask what these investments *actually* represent. These aren't vanity projects, investment opportunities to make the line go up or the numbers get bigger; rather, every single one of our investments is a step closer to one of the Four Freedoms. I would argue that the tried and true American vision of retirement at age sixty-five is outdated and a horrible way to live your life. If you love what you're doing, and have enough money to support your lifestyle, why would you stop working? Conversely, why work for forty years at something you didn't like and then just stop? Most of the people we see do this actually wither with this formula as their worlds just get smaller. They lose purpose and start to move into a scarcity mindset about their health and wealth. Why not take control *now* and ensure an extraordinary life of fulfillment?

Here's how you can get away from the typical psychology of money that most of us start off with: reconceptualize your money as oxygen as I recommend in the first chapter. Remember the oxygen analogy: money is what allows you to live, not what you live for. Let that be the guiding thought process behind your financial decisions. Then, before making any financial decision, consider how it will get you closer to one or more of the Four Freedoms.

THE FOUR FREEDOMS™

The term "financial freedom" shows up often in investing circles. It's a great term that quickly expresses what many of us want our money to do. The more it's used, though, the easier it becomes to get hyper-fixated on the word "financial" and lose sight of the word "freedom." That's why the conception of money as oxygen is so important to creating a wealth-building mindset: you have to remember that it's the freedom that you want more than the money to get it.

Dan Sullivan, creator of The Strategic Coach® Program, has identified four freedoms that allow entrepreneurs to experience greater simplicity and clarity. No one freedom is more important than another, but you may find that you and your family need to prioritize one or two over the others. As long as you keep yourself moving forward in any of these directions, you'll end up much closer to holistic wealth. (To learn more, visit this link: https://resources.strategiccoach.com/the-multiplier-mindset-blog/putting-the-focus-on-freedom.)

FREEDOM OF PURPOSE

The Freedom of Purpose is the freedom to do as you want. It's the ability to live your life the way you want to *without worry*. If you're reading this book, you're probably able to do a certain amount of things you want to do, but probably not able to do all of them (or maybe even any of them) without some amount of worry.

FREEDOM OF MONEY

The Freedom of Money is the freedom to live your life focusing on what you want to be doing with your time and not being beholden to a paycheck. Freedom of Money includes having money to spend, but it more so refers to the freedom of being able to live intentionally by spending your time in a way that aligns with your vision.

FREEDOM OF TIME

The Freedom of Time is the freedom to spend your professional and personal life doing what it is that fascinates and motivates you. Many people, regardless of their financial situation, feel stuck in a job they're not happy in. This becomes pervasive in their personal lives as well, and a lack of fulfillment prevails.

FREEDOM OF RELATIONSHIP

The Freedom of Relationship is the freedom to work with, and work only with, the people you want to. This Freedom is often swept aside in favor of the other three, but it's just as important. I have met many people who sacrifice this freedom in order to build their wealth, and they always end up miserable, spending the majority of their time with people they don't like.

CREATING YOUR VISION STATEMENT

Many of my clients come to me ready to dive immediately into the details of their investment opportunities. But I always encourage them to slow down a bit. Before I discuss alternative assets or infinite banking with them, I insist they make a vision statement. That's true for you, too. Now you can begin thinking about how to create the wealth needed to experience your life the way you want to.

You've probably created vision statements before, either for yourself or a business. This one will be a little different. By answering the questions below, you will create a vision statement that lays out the dreams you have for yourself. I use the word "dreams" here because it's important that, whatever your goals are, you're excited for and even tantalized by them. You're about to do some hard work to achieve these goals— you need to make sure they are absolutely spellbinding.

The vision statement is also important because, as with any goal, if you don't have a target, you're likely to miss it every time. You might know that you want to make more money, but until you know *why* you want to make more money and *why* you're excited about the things that money can get you, it will be easy to lose the inspiration to keep trying. Then, further in the process, you might get off track and lose sight of your long-term goals. When that happens, you need to have something tangible to come back to. That tangible something is a vision statement.

There are many different ways to make a statement like this, but starting from a calm, clear, neutral place leads to the best results. If you start drafting your vision statement right after a stressful day at the office, for instance, you might end up including "quit my job" as one of your goals when really you just want to be more respected at work. This is what I suggest you do:

Travel to an inspirational destination, turn off your phone, exercise, meditate, and close your eyes. Take a breath. In order to answer these questions, you have to be in a deep state of focus and clarity. It's okay if you struggle at first to seriously answer each of these questions—you can always try again later when you're more focused. The important thing is that you're really taking the time to do this kind of dreamlining. There will be times to rush later on in your journey, but this is not one of them.

Once you've cleared out your mind of any distractions, ask yourself the following questions. These are the simplest, most concise way to think about your life's aspirations, and the answers to them should be as well. That doesn't mean you should forgo putting everything important in the vision statement, but you should shoot for something that you can easily imagine and realize any time you need a little inspiration.

- If you had all the money in the world, where would you be? What would you be doing? Who would you be with?

This one is pretty self-explanatory, but it's vital to ask. For example, you might be dreaming with your spouse that you want to leave your day job behind, move to and live on a tropical island, and become the novelist you always aspired to be but that seemed impossible to reach. Your spouse is with you and built a dream house with several guest rooms to accommodate all of your friends and family to spend time with. This will form the basis of your vision for wealth, so being honest about your desires will save you a ton of time and headaches later on. Try to keep your answers concise, but don't sacrifice any details or goals in an attempt to make things more "manageable."

- Are there any beliefs from your past that are limiting your potential today?

We'll discuss this concept in more detail in Chapter 4, so you may end up revisiting this question after you read it. The key thing to realize is that you must not only identify your limiting beliefs, but you must face them head-on and challenge their veracity.

It's likely that you won't even know a belief is limiting until you begin examining your thoughts about money and investing. Begin by thinking about all the conventional wisdom you've accrued over the years and seriously reanalyze it. Is putting all of your money into your company 401k plan really the best thing to do? Is deferring taxes to your later years the wisest thing to do? Why? Is your reason truly rational or are you just holding onto a limiting belief? In that way, think of the things your financial advisors, your parents, your friends, or your colleagues have told you about financial planning and decide if you really want to hold these values going forward.

If it seems impossible to hold one of these beliefs at the same time as you move forward with your goals, then ditch it.

- Are the people in your circle, the media you consume, or the environment you are in driving you toward your vision or pulling you away?

This can be a hard pill to swallow, but it's essential to recognize the things in your life that are keeping you back. If someone is regularly telling you to do less, to play it safe, or to rein in your ambitions, regardless of who that person is, you probably don't want them to be impacting the big decisions you make in your life. The same is true for the kind of news you read, shows you watch, and spaces you spend most of your time in. There's a difference between caution and negativity, and you can trust yourself to determine which is which. But you must inventory the feeds of information you are receiving—whether it's coming from your cousin with the finance degree or a talking head on TV, be mindful of what's coming to you. You want to have an abundance mindset, not a scarcity mindset. Is it in support of your creation of real wealth or working against it?

- Is the current state of your health generating energy and conditioning your mind toward achieving your vision?

There is no amount of wealth that will make you feel good in your body, and you won't be able to attain any of the Four Freedoms if you don't have the energy and well-being to be a full participant in your own life. I'll go into more detail about the importance of health in the next chapter; for now, taking a cursory glance at your health will suffice.

- Are you living intentionally with ever-expanding goals and high-performing habits to achieve them?

If you're living intentionally, that means you are mindful of what you're doing and where you are at all times. It means you never live by rote or in a cycle of tried-and-true habits. You'll want to check in on this question periodically, as new habits will evolve and grow over time that may be beneficial at first, but after long use could become stagnant cycles. Well after you start your journey to holistic wealth, you will need to keep assessing your growth and ensuring that you are headed in a forward-moving direction. If you find yourself resting on the wealth you've created, using it to stagnate and do less in your life, I assure you that you will quickly run out of enthusiasm for the life you've worked extremely hard to achieve.

When I cover this last question with my clients, they often realize that a number of the things they're dreaming of they can already obtain. I found myself in such a place recently when I revisited my vision statement. I realized that I wanted to see my parents two times a year. That's a pretty obtainable goal for me—I just need to take a little bit of time off work and spend a few hours in the air. I don't need to make any new investments nor do I need to greatly rearrange my life to make that happen. This exercise revealed to me that I actually already have the freedom I need to spend time with my parents, but I was missing the awareness that I had it.

* * *

Thinking deeply and dreaming freely about your vision can be an overwhelming experience if you get bogged down in the *how* of doing it all. But figuring out *how* is not the reason to answer the questions. Remember, they are about finding your *why*. If you focus on the end goal, on your enthusiasm to obtain it, this exercise can be a very empowering experience.

In school and frequently in life, we're taught that we shouldn't dream, that we should just focus on what we can practically do and affect right now. But dreaming is precisely how we figure out what it is that we really want. If you want to build your wealth, you do so by starting with getting clarity in your vision statement.

MEASURE BACKWARD, NOT AGAINST THE IDEAL

We humans are hardwired to compare ourselves to other people. When my clients begin this kind of vision building, a common place for them to start is by looking at people they see as living an ideal life. Looking at successful people can be a helpful way to learn about the kinds of things or behaviors you want to incorporate into your life—doing just that was a huge part of my quest to learn about wealth-building—but comparing your success to anyone else's inherently doesn't make sense. Doing so can distort your own vision-building process and throw you off course from your goals.

When evaluating your success and growth, measure against where you were, not where you want to be. If you start going to the gym, those first few weeks are going to be exceedingly hard on your body, and you may even feel farther from your health goals than when you started. But at the end of those first weeks, if you compare yourself to where you were and not to where you want to be, you'll see a massive amount of improvement. The same is true with financial success. By measuring backward we are able to gain positive momentum from our accomplishments that propel us into the future. This courage creates confidence, which in turn creates new capabilities, which is the lifecycle of growth. Of course, if you don't see any improvement, then you will need to change something or spend more time doing this or that, but you're never going to realize what changes you need to make if you are constantly comparing yourself to the idealized version of where you want to be. Further, you will never live up to those idealistic expectations that put you in a state of living in what Dan Sullivan calls The Gap™. That's why I always advise my clients to measure backward. This is how you get your dreams to inspire you, not intimidate you from chasing them.

THE BOTTOM LINE: TAKE TIME TO THINK AND DREAM

Thinking deeply and dreaming freely is hard work. Whoever came up with the idea of the lackadaisical, head-in-the-clouds dreamer never tried to seriously confront what it is they wanted to achieve. This kind of imagining is an absolutely essential step on the path toward extraordinary wealth. You might find it difficult to clearly articulate what it is you want, either because you have limiting beliefs about the possibility of getting there or because you're afraid of not living up to your ideal self. I've helped dozens of people figure out their goals, and while I've seen the process be difficult, I've seen the incredible effect it has on the lives of the people who take it on. Do yourself a favor and think a little bigger and dream a little more. Your future self will thank you for your vision.

When I started learning about the psychology of money, I was shocked to find out how little time Americans spend thinking about their financial future. The well-trod path to success has conditioned us to outsource this most important activity, leading many of us to think only about our finances in the most shallow sense. Thinking deeply about and dreaming freely about The Four Freedoms™ and the life you want to live is not just an essential step toward increasing your wealth portfolio—it's an active way to take control of your money back and live a life of purpose and prosperity.

* * *

You've seen my journey, you've learned about the three biggest wealth disrupters, you've learned about the psychology of money and The Four Freedoms™, and now you've actually drafted a vision statement. You've already come a lot farther than most people ever do, and if you've been paying attention and being really honest with yourself about what you want to achieve, then you've laid the foundation for real wealth. Now, it's time to start building it.

The traditional roadmap to success tells us to reach a number in our retirement account and then give up. You and I both know this isn't nearly good enough, but still—that kind of conventional thinking can be extremely hard to break out of. In the next chapter, the beginning of the second section of the book, I'll teach you how to change your mindset and really begin raising the level of your Financial IQ. By leveling up in this way, you'll be able to head into a future that's always bigger than your past.

PART 2

PURSUING REAL WEALTH

Chapter 4

PHASE 1: YOUR MINDSET

THERE IS NO HURDLE TOO BIG THAT A BIGGER MINDSET CAN'T CLEAR

YOU

MINDSET
- Your Why
- Growth Mindset
- Beliefs
- Health
- Habits
- Goals

VISION STATEMENT ⟶

Ever wonder why wealthy people who have a misfortune and hit bankruptcy are able to climb right back out of it and get back to even higher heights? It's because they have a growth mindset and understand the strategy for building wealth. Once you master your mindset and the game of capitalism, the numbers only get bigger. As a case in point, meet my daughter.

My oldest daughter is incredible with her money. She's responsible with how she spends it, yes, but she's also already aggressively leveraging this wealth strategy to achieve her life goals—which she's spent no small amount of time dreaming up. At twenty-three, she and her fiancé leveraged her infinite banking policy for the down payment on her first house and now have over $100,000 in equity. They have since turned the place into a cash-flowing rental property and purchased their second property. There aren't many young people who take such an active role in their finances and even fewer who leverage it the way she does. I couldn't be more proud to see her implement this strategy for herself to achieve her dreams.

Her peers, however, aren't like her. They're not irresponsible with their money, and they've grown up with a host of limiting beliefs about what it can do. Their parents have a typical middle-class mindset that says you should put as much money into a 401k as possible and that all debt, even debt that can readily be paid off or used as an asset, is bad. In turn, the younger people have picked up these same beliefs and refuse to let go of them, and they're often disapproving of my daughter's financial decisions. They're all good, smart kids who know a thing or two about managing their finances. The difference between them is that my daughter has a Growth Mindset and her peers do not.

I don't blame my daughter's peers for not having developed a Growth Mindset. There is a $30 trillion financial services industry in this country that has been actively controlling the message that you are not smart enough to manage your own finances. That industry does not set us up for success; in fact, it's built on the idea that we can't develop our own mindsets to manage our money. If we could—and we can—then there'd be no need for this financial advising industry. And let me tell you, there isn't a need for that industry.

You don't have to settle for that conventional wisdom and way of thinking. The mindset put forth by that industry will help you become and stay middle-class, but it won't get you the kind of wealth you know you're capable of building. In order to experience true wealth, you need to cultivate your Growth Mindset. This will get you much closer to the Four Freedoms I mentioned in the last chapter, and you will also find that this mindset will improve basically every aspect of your life. With a Growth Mindset in place, you'll be able to experience life more richly, form new ideas, create stronger relationships, and adopt the habits to foster them.

Hence, the first and most critical stage of the Wealth Framework is your mindset and belief system. If you do not believe you can master your mind, then this strategy is likely not for you. If you have already made progress or are open to learning and having a Growth Mindset, then congratulations, and let's get started on expanding from where you are.

THE FOUR ELEMENTS OF CULTIVATING A GROWTH MINDSET

There are four key elements to forming a Growth Mindset. The first element is learning. In order to grow, you have to stay open to learning and constantly take in new ideas. Even if you don't end up using them, and even if you fundamentally disagree with them, you need to have a mindset that allows for new ideas to easily be considered.

The second element is letting go of limiting beliefs. In Chapter 2, I talked about wealth disrupters and how conventional wisdom gets in the way of people's financial goals. Developing a mindset that comfortably disposes of unhelpful but entrenched thinking will accelerate your journey toward real wealth.

The third element is building dynamic relationships. You are ultimately the product of the five people you spend the most time with, so in order to level up your Growth Mindset, you need to make sure that you're spending your limited time with people who really challenge, inspire, and engage you. If you're not surrounded by high-quality relationships, you are not going to develop a high-quality mindset.

The fourth element is making good habits. If you are not able to incorporate certain best practices into your life, within and outside the sphere of financial planning, you will not be able to act on the kind of success you can expect from following the rest of the advice in this book. Good habits are the basis of a good life, which is ultimately what you are going on this entire financial journey for.

I'll show you how to develop each of these elements to develop a robust Growth Mindset. I wrote this book to help you achieve your financial goals, but if you follow my advice and form a great Growth Mindset, you will experience life in a fuller, richer, more stimulating way than before. You owe that to more than just your portfolio: you owe it to yourself.

LEARNING CONSTANTLY

How many people do you meet who think that they know it all? If you're any kind of professional, the answer is probably many people. When you go through years of education, as most professionals do, and then once you've spent one or two decades climbing the ranks of your given field, it's very easy to start believing that you know it all and know better than anyone else. This is a natural outcropping of expertise, and while I encourage you to try to know it all, I strongly discourage you from believing that you actually do.

The truth is that we are meant to learn all throughout our life, and the sooner you decide to stop learning and just coast on your accumulated knowledge, the harder it becomes to reactivate those portions of your mind. You're reading this book because you feel stagnated in your financial progress. If you don't have it already, you need to develop a mindset that prioritizes learning in order to achieve your wealth goals. And if you are already there, then you know that all of us are served well by taking the time to improve it.

Having a Growth Mindset doesn't mean you'll agree with everything you hear or see. That would just be naivety. It means actively listening to new information and considering if it has a use to you. I know so many people who, when they hear the kind of advice I advocate for, just shut down and shut out of the conversation because it contradicts the longstanding beliefs they have about money. I have no problem with people who disagree with what I advocate for—I find that my track record and my list of satisfied clients speak for themselves—but I do have an issue with people who won't even consider what I have to say or how they could incorporate parts of it into their wealth building. By the end of this book, well after you've developed a Growth Mindset, I fully expect you to do more research and listen to other experts on how to achieve your financial goals. If you don't, if you think that this book is the end of your journey and not the beginning, then I haven't successfully advocated for a Growth Mindset.

It can be difficult to figure out if you have a mindset geared toward learning, but a good place to start is to think about how you behave when you meet someone new. If you're at a cocktail party, what do you do when someone starts talking to you? Do you ask questions about who they are, what they do, or how they do it? When they bring up a topic you don't know much about, do you engage with it and ask them to tell you more? Or do you change the topic to something you know about? I've been to plenty of cocktail parties where no one has much of interest to say, but I always make sure to listen actively to the people I meet. Everyone has something to teach, but you'll never learn those things unless you're open to it.

You have to be honest with yourself during an exercise like this. No one wants to admit that they're checked out in most of the conversations they have, but if you can't name the things that someone else has taught you in the past year or however long, then you need to reevaluate how you're engaging with new ideas. I find that reading is a tremendous source of new ideas. By setting a daily reading habit you can significantly increase the number of books you read per year.

LETTING GO OF LIMITING BELIEFS

Once an idea gets in our heads, it's difficult to get it out. At twenty-three, my daughter's peers have already completely subscribed to the conventional roadmap to success. On one hand, that's a testament to how seriously they think about their finances and how intelligent they are that they can do that kind of long-term planning. But on the other hand, it's illustrative of the way that unhelpful ideas can take root in our minds at a young age. Her peers' limiting beliefs are so entrenched that, when my daughter brings up alternative investing or infinite banking, some of her friends completely shut down or spin her advice into an argument.

It's not easy figuring out which of your beliefs are limiting: it took me twenty years to uproot the most pernicious of them in my quest to achieve extraordinary wealth. I advise all my clients to think about the bedrock of their investing knowledge. This is where they find the axioms like "diversification in the stock market," "defer your taxes in a 401k," "pay off your mortgage quicker" and the like. Before long these beliefs become ingrained in our thoughts and actions. I encourage my clients to ask when they adopted these ideas. When they think about it, they often tell me that they've held those beliefs for most of their lives without even realizing it.

Many of the core beliefs that we hold are ones we picked up decades ago. A lot has changed in the world since we incorporated those beliefs into our ways of thinking, and the chance that we need to update them is quite high. After asking yourself the same question (when did you adopt those beliefs), if you find that the majority of your financial beliefs were made ten, twenty, even thirty years ago, it's likely you're holding on to a number of limiting beliefs. If you're really curious to learn and actually excited to grow your wealth,

ıen you have the intellectual tools to objectively analyze
these beliefs are really working for you or the other way
around.

BUILDING DYNAMIC RELATIONSHIPS

It's very common for me to get clients who are doing everything right on paper. They're shirking their limiting beliefs,
they're articulating how they'll achieve The Four Freedoms™,
and they're keen to make ambitious alternative investments.
Yet there's something holding them back, some voice in their
head that urges them to proceed with caution when really
they need to move aggressively forward. More often than not,
that's an external voice from a relationship that's hurting their
Growth Mindset.

You can have the best Growth Mindset in the world, and it
won't mean anything if the people you spend your time with
aren't interested in your or their growth. If you look at the
amount of time you spend with people, you'll find that the
majority of that time is spent with just a handful of individuals.
Your family, certainly, probably some coworkers, and maybe a
few friends. That means that all the social information you're
taking in is coming from a very select group of individuals.
Since we know that humans are susceptible to groupthink, it's
also very likely that those people are, in one way or another,
parroting each other's beliefs. In a social environment like that,
it's almost impossible to avoid limiting beliefs and mindsets
antithetical to growth.

I'm not advocating for you to ditch your friends or family, but
I do suggest that you think seriously about who you spend

your limited free time with. This is especially true for platonic, social relationships. If you spend every weekend watching football and eating nachos with your friends, the chances of you developing a healthy diet are significantly lower than if you spent that same time with your rock climbing buddies. Relaxation and leisure are extremely important parts of life, but if you're not spending your time with people who stimulate you, you should really consider how much time you want to spend with those people.

My best friend, Keith, is a tremendous individual on many fronts, including being a master yogi and avid cyclist. That's what we bonded over: we both bike about 150 miles every week, train with the same coach, and have competed in countless cycling events. Keith's sixty-eight years old, an accomplished psychiatrist, an entrepreneur with his own business, and a Stanford grad, so he has a completely different perspective on things from me. When we get together, we talk about all kinds of things: neurobiology, health, psychology, finance—all kinds of stuff. He's a great guy, and I consider him my best friend in no small part because of the way he exposes me to new ideas.

Keith is a large part of my Growth Mindset. So are my wife and other entrepreneurs in my mastermind communities. This isn't just because they're the people that I'm stuck with; rather, they're the people I decided to build my life with and around. I can point to a number of ways these people have influenced my obsessive quest for true wealth, but in truth, their impact on me and my journey is inarticulable. This book, this wealth of knowledge I've accumulated over the years, is as much a product of my personal journey with wealth as it is a reflection of the countless conversations I've had with all of these people. If they weren't such dynamic, smart, stimulating people, there's no way I'd be where I am today.

MAKING GOOD HABITS

If you are not following up on these elements of building a Growth Mindset with good habits, you will never see the rewards that such a mindset can reap. If learning and letting go of limiting beliefs are the theories behind the Growth Mindset, then making good habits is the practice.

"Good habits" is an intentionally vague term: what works for you might not work for me, etc. At the core of any good habit, however, is demonstrable evidence of the improvement of your life. Just because you're regularly doing something doesn't mean that it's a good habit.

As you're figuring out what habits you need to adopt, think about what areas of your growth mindset you want to grow. For example, I set aside time every night to read about the latest entrepreneurial or wealth insight. I host my own podcast, *Wealth Strategy Secrets of the Ultra-Wealthy*, and get to interview some of the biggest thought leaders in the wealth-building space. I also listen to other wealth-building podcasts all the time, am a member of exclusive mastermind communities for the ultra-wealthy, and attend conferences to constantly expand my own Financial IQ. Doing these things takes time among many competing priorities, but it is what fascinates and motivates me. By creating the space I need to always be learning, these habits are a vital part of how I maintain my Growth Mindset.

I'm also passionate about my health. I exercise every day, and I eat a clean, fresh diet. I make sure I get plenty of sleep every night. I do this because I need a high-functioning body and mind in order to build the kind of wealth that I want. No one really thinks about the health component of building real wealth, but the truth is, what I have done and what I suggest you and my clients should do takes a ton of energy—energy that, at fifty-two, I wouldn't generate without being in peak performance.

I have so many clients working seventy-hour weeks because they think that's how they're going to build real wealth (a limiting belief: you have to earn what you're worth!) when the reality is that they are wearing themselves so thin that any wealth they can generate is completely negated by their physical capacity to experience it. You cannot have real, holistic wealth without a bedrock of health. The only way you are going to form that kind of health is if you prioritize it as a core habit.

Of course, your health is just one area where you can create better habits. In Chapter 5, I'll go into a little more detail about the kinds of habits I encourage my clients to create to support their Mindset IQ.

THE BOTTOM LINE: GROWTH IS STIMULATION

A Growth Mindset can be most easily broken down into the four elements, but it really boils down to allowing yourself to be constantly stimulated by new information. In a Growth Mindset, you are always cycling new ideas in and out of your mind, challenging old assumptions, and replacing them with new ways of thinking. You're reading this book because you feel stagnant, stuck in a holding pattern with your finances: you need to vary your mindset in order to break out of it. Before you make any ambitious investments or shake up your portfolio, you have to adopt a way of thinking that will position you to take advantage of new ideas as they come to you. This is a Growth Mindset: actively staying open to the dynamism of the world around you.

At just twenty-three, my daughter's already building an extraordinary life for herself. That's because she has a powerful Growth Mindset. It's incredible to see someone so young so unburdened by the limiting beliefs it took me twenty years or more to let go of. It will take some of her friends a little bit longer to come around to our way of seeing things, but if she's serious about those friendships, they, too, will soon begin to experience the rewards of a Growth Mindset. If you seriously reflect on your life and take it back into your own hands, I assure you that you, too, can develop a mindset that will take you toward a life of your dreams.

* * *

Education is a prominent feature of the Growth Mindset, and in the next chapter, I'll define for you the Three Foundational IQs you need to have in order to think critically and learn ferociously about your finances. As you reignite your learning process, you can think about which of the Three IQs you need to focus on developing and how. From here on out, you're going to be learning a lot about wealth, so it's vital that you organize your "study plan," as it were. Understanding the Three Foundational IQs will empower you to do that.

Chapter 5

PHASE 2: BUILD THE THREE FOUNDATIONAL IQS

INVESTING IN YOUR FUTURE SELF

**LEARNING &
TEAM BUILDING**

YOU

**FINANCIAL IQ
MINDSET IQ
HEALTH IQ**
- Invest in yourself
- Challenge existing biases
- Learn new strategies

MINDSET
- Your Why
- Growth Mindset
- Beliefs
- Health
- Habits
- Goals

VISION STATEMENT ──────────────────────────────────────▶

I have a goal to live to 116. That might seem overly ambitious, but with rapid advancements in medical technology and the proactive steps I'm taking now to be healthy and wealthy, I think it's totally possible. Furthermore, it has changed my mindset about age and mentally, I feel more my biological age than my chronological age.

When people enter their old age, they start running out of money. These are the years when people spend their nest eggs and stop bringing new money in. As they're quitting work, they don't have anywhere to go or much to do, and their friends are starting to pass away, so their communities shrink. Older people are more susceptible to disease and illness, sure, but it's no wonder that people with little to live for end up passing away quickly.

A big part of my health plan to live to 116 is to make sure that I continue working for as long as I can and that I constantly grow my social circles. This goes back to the Growth Mindset, though in this case, its value comes not from its ability to grow a wealth portfolio but rather from its ability to grow my own capacity.

Because I have an ambitious goal for how long I want to live, I have a cutting-edge doctor on my team who specializes in integrative medicine. At a regular checkup, this doctor found that one of my arteries was 55 percent blocked. I was shocked; I thought that since I exercised at an elite level, regularly focused on nutrition, and was proactive with my health, I was less susceptible to these kinds of conditions. This was a huge wake-up call for me. I'd just spent the past twenty or so years learning as much as I could about being wealthy only for all of that to be jeopardized by a single blocked artery.

That's when I realized that you need to be the key asset on which everything else is built. If you don't develop your financial knowledge, your personal mindset, and your health, you will never be holistically wealthy. You can make the best investments in the world and position your wealth as strategically as possible, but if you haven't seriously invested time, money, and development into yourself, you are not going to lead a life of abundance.

* * *

At my private equity firm, unlike other, traditional firms that are purely focused on particular products, we provide value to our clients through the Pantheon Advantage. In that way, we help our clients develop a truly holistic approach to building their wealth and living their vision. Without having this, clients end up either unable to see returns on their investments or in lifestyles that cannot act on the freedom their expanded portfolios would offer them.

That's why you need to build up each of the Three Foundational IQs: Financial IQ, Mindset IQ, and Health IQ. Just like the Four Freedoms, no singular IQ is more important than the other, but you may find that you need to work on developing one over the other. I always remind my clients that just because these concepts are new to them doesn't mean they lack some key skills to develop these IQs. This stuff just isn't taught in college or grad school, despite it being totally instrumental to every decision we make in our lives. If you read this chapter and absorb what I have to tell you, you will gain a trove of intellectual tools that you can use to build up your wealth, improve your critical thinking, and suffuse your life with holistically healthy practices. By developing the Three Foundational IQs, you will make a massive, tangible investment in yourself.

THE THREE FOUNDATIONAL IQS

The best way to think of each of the Three Foundational IQs is as a toolkit. In these toolkits, you'll find all kinds of institutional knowledge, strategies, and guidelines, as well as a series of best practices and good habits that you can adopt today to improve anything from your portfolio to your way of thinking. You'll also find counterintuitive definitions and different ways to think about commonly held (and limiting) beliefs. These IQs are going to be your touchstones, the deep wells of knowledge you can come back to when you need a little more insight or confidence in the financial moves you're making.

FINANCIAL IQ

My friend Maria and I talk a lot about finances. We're both interested in and passionate about money, so our conversations always end up revolving around finance. Whenever I talk money with Maria, I urge her to start investing in commercial real estate—one of my favorite alternative investments. Without fail, she always sighs and rolls her eyes because she knows Daniel, her husband, will never go in for it. It's great that they make their financial decisions together, but sometimes I really wish she would plow forward on her own.

A few years ago, Daniel decided to invest in a single-family rental property, and like many people in that situation, he had a terrible experience with the tenant. After that and a few other issues with the property, Daniel felt so burned by the mere concept of investing in real estate that he totally shuts down at the mention of real estate investment.

Daniel is a great example of someone who doesn't have a

Growth Mindset, both because he's bogged down in limiting beliefs and because he refuses to incorporate new ideas into his way of thinking. But when I think about Daniel, I think more about how much he'd benefit from developing his Financial IQ—that is, if he took the steps outlined in this book (or in others) and learned as much as he could about taking control of his finances.

I shouldn't be so hard on Daniel—this kind of financial advice, earthshaking to the traditional roadmap to success, takes a while to sink in. I can appreciate that caution when it comes to money, but among my clients, the ones who wholeheartedly adopt the strategies they discover as they expand their Financial IQ are the ones who benefit the most from what Pantheon has to offer. I have a client who, within a year of working with us, divested completely from the stock market and sold off his 401k. He went fully into alternative assets and multifamily real estate investment, and now he's seeing 20 to 50 percent returns on his investments. That's a truly life-altering amount of money. It's important to think deeply about your financial decisions, but with so many stories of success with alternative investing out there, the time to jump in is now.

"Alternative" Investments

Let's back up for a second and talk about the word "alternative." I use this word a lot when I'm talking about the kind of investments that I advocate for, but I use it a little bit subversively. The financial services industry has labeled these as alternative investments primarily because they don't offer them. Commercial properties or multifamily real estate syndications, oil and gas, self-storage, mobile home parks, agriculture, notes, life settlements—the list goes on. The only thing "alternative" about these investments is that they aren't the bread and butter of the financial advising industry: they're actually quite sound, they are tangible assets, and they are historically profitable.

Consider the irony of property investment, for instance, being labeled as "alternative." That's in comparison to the cryptic, constantly shifting, unpredictable nature of the stock market. The $20 trillion financial services industry labels the very bedrock of the American Dream—owning property—as an "alternative" way to grow your wealth. Since it doesn't make them any money, it is an "alternative" investment for them. And I'm OK with that. A big part of developing your Financial IQ is understanding what alternative investments are out there and why they are considered to be "alternative" in the first place.

You started improving your Financial IQ when you began reading your book. And if you've created your vision statement, then you've taken two steps. Other steps will be found in the rest of this book. They include:

- Create an overall wealth strategy that supports your vision.
- Develop a comprehensive tax strategy and reduce your biggest expense.
- Become your own bank with infinite banking.
- Build a fortress around your wealth, family, and legacy.
- Invest in tangible assets.

Outside of those, you build your Financial IQ the way you build any intelligence: actively learn. Listen to podcasts, read as many books as you can, join mastermind groups, and surround yourself with people who are expanding their Financial IQ. The point is, don't let yourself reach a point where you think you know enough. There will always be something else to learn: learn it.

There are still two other Foundational IQs to discuss, and these are the toolkits that will actually empower you to make the best use of the tools you gain from developing your Financial IQ.

MINDSET IQ

As you should know by now, if you don't have your mindset right, it doesn't matter how good the investment is: you are not going to experience real wealth. I have a friend with $200,000 sitting in a savings account. That's a significant amount of money, but he doesn't do anything at all with it. With inflation currently at 8.5 percent, he's completely losing value. Because his mindset is so limited, he's not able to access nearly any of the wealth the bare facts of his portfolio would suggest that he has.

There are books out there like *The Millionaire Next Door*, that will tell you to scrimp and save as much as possible in order to accrue some outlandish and appealing number, like $1 million. These books will tell you to cut out your morning Starbucks run, only eat at home, and stop buying new furniture just so you can squirrel away an arbitrary sum of money. I won't stop anyone from saving money or cutting corners, but at a certain point, you have to ask yourself: what is the point of all that? You can go through years of toil and frugality to get a certain amount of money, but are you really going to be able to use that money to live a better life? Probably not, if you've spent the majority of your life in a scarcity mindset that deprioritizes happiness.

At Pantheon, we advocate for a life of abundance. That means having as much money as you need to live the lifestyle you desire *and* a bunch of joy to spare. There's no point in setting a financial goal for yourself if reaching it means that you have to suffer. With clever investing and smart use of the tax code, you simply do not need to ruin your life to build real wealth. This is why you need to develop your Mindset IQ. If you're not thinking about the life you want your wealth to build for you, you are never going to have true wealth.

I know people who have made $5, $10, or even $20 million exits and still worry about ending up destitute. All their lives, they've only considered that money comes from hard work, from labor of some sort, so they can't imagine their money working for them. They have inefficient 401ks and saving plans that slowly fritter away their wealth, and they worry all the way through retirement until it's over (in death).

Those people obviously have some kind of Financial IQ. They aren't making the best investments, but they know how to accrue wealth. Still, their Mindset IQ is diminished. They cannot view their wealth as something that will grow and sustain them. They can't imagine it doing anything other than being a number on a spreadsheet. Without a developed Mindset IQ, they really don't have anything.

Probably the most valuable thing in the Mindset IQ toolkit is goal-setting practices. Setting clear and exciting goals for yourself is the best way to cut through the malaise that comes to so many of us when we think about money. If you can constantly check in on what you want your money to do for you, then you will always know how you need to use it.

My goal-setting practice helps me keep control of my life. You can use mine as a model for yourself, but you have to make your own. My goals are not going to look like your goals, so why should our practices geared toward reaching them look the same? I never tell my clients what goals they should have; instead, I tell them the general ways that they can form their own.

I review my goals on a weekly basis. As long as you're reviewing your goals semi-regularly, any schedule is fine. I like to take my Friday mornings off just to look at my goals. Before I look at my email or take any phone calls, on Friday mornings I evaluate where I'm at and where I want to be. Doing this before I go into a "reactive" state—where I'm just responding to my daily obligations—really helps me focus. Every week I'm positioned to make decisions informed by the goals that I have, not the day's stresses, and I also have a chance to realign based on my observations on the week before.

The human mind likes to think in 90-day blocks. That's just a basic tenet of how our brains work, so the first check-in point for any goal should always be 90 days out. After that, one year, three years, ten years, and twenty-five years out are good guideposts that will give you a range to think about. It's important to dream about your financial goals, so let those later points really inspire you and give you something to head toward.

You should also think about what needs to happen personally and professionally for you to feel happy with your results. When you really consider that, it cuts through all the noise that accumulates around goal setting. Your goals should be ambitious and exciting, but make sure you set yourself up for success and not disappointment by identifying the things you need to do in order to feel like you're on track.

High-Performance Habits

To actually reach those goals, you need to set a series of high-performance habits. This goes back directly to developing your Growth Mindset. I won't specify what habits you need to make for yourself—you have to figure that out—but I will show you how to think about and categorize them. Brendan Burchard's book *The High-Performance Habits* lays out six types of habits that can directly improve your ability to reach the goals you set: clarity, energy, necessity, productivity, influence, and courage. It's an incredible book, and I recommend that you read it for yourself—it'll really shape how you think about your behavior.

The first high-performance habit is clarity. How often do you find yourself in a conflicted state? With a question that broad, the answer surely is—often. Most married people come to a point where they disagree with their partner about how to use their money. My wife and I are on the same page about so much of this stuff, but even we have found ourselves disagreeing about money. Because we both practice clarity as a habit, however, nine times out of ten we're able to slow down before getting into an argument and evaluate what is important to us. Articulated in terms of our goals, we usually find that we don't disagree about much at all: we just have slightly different ideas about how to get the things we both want. Conflict is a normal occurrence in life, and learning how to preempt it with clarity is essential to performing at a higher level.

Energy is the next high-performance habit. Whatever you do, do it with passion, excitement, and energy—that's the essence of the energy habit. So many of my clients are experiencing burnout in their lives, which leads them to feel like they need to expend *less* energy when in reality they need to expend *more*. If you aren't feeling energized doing the things you love, the things you want to accomplish, or even the things you are obligated to do, then you either need to change what you're doing or change how you're doing them. Life is too short to slump through it: only do things that energize you or that you can bring your full level of energy to. You might need to build other habits to feed the energy you need to be bringing to your life (I'll talk more about this in the next section), but remember that it's always better to do one thing fully than to do several things at half-capacity. If you find yourself exhausted in your work or your leisure activities, start thinking of that as a problem to be solved and not a downside to ignore.

As a habit, necessity has a lot in common with energy, but it's more about the internal drive than it is external fuel. Necessity ensures that everything you do comes from a place of need. To really perform at a high level, you have to feel like what you are doing—professionally and personally—is important. If you make necessity a habit, you won't miss calls or call in sick or blow off your responsibilities; instead, you'll clamor to do as much as you can in the limited time that you have.

After that is productivity. In this environment after COVID, it seems like everyone is working all the time, but very few of us are actually getting anything done. We might be on call at the computer all day, but we're also taking care of the kids and making dinner and everything else. Everything we do in a day has a tendency to jumble up on top of each other, so that, instead of knocking out one task at a time, we end up doing a little bit of everything all at once. The best way to actualize the productivity habit is to block out your time and be serious about only keeping the things you scheduled for within those blocks. It's tempting to reschedule that meeting for the weekend or to put off those emails until the next day, but if you want to be truly productive and intentional about your life, you have to stick to the time you set for yourself.

The next habit is influence. Everyone, no matter their profession, is selling something. Every interaction between people can be broken down into some kind of exchange, with one person wanting something from the other or wanting to give the other person something. In order to take full advantage of your time and skills, you need to hone your influence. You can also think of this as charisma—it certainly presents itself that way in some of the world's most powerful and wealthy individuals. This habit is oriented around finding your capacity to influence others and bringing it to the fore of all your interactions.

The final habit is courage. This goes back to the importance of learning. You need to have the courage to constantly challenge yourself to do better, to work harder. If you don't make courage a habit, you are going to stagnate and only do the things you think that you can achieve instead of going for the things you really want. You cannot exist just in your comfort zone if you want to perform at a high level.

All of these habits and goal-setting are geared toward taking control of your life. I keep coming back to this because it is simply the most important thing for you to do. A developed Mindset IQ is a toolkit specifically tailored to getting you back in control of your life. If you're constantly dreaming, setting bigger and bigger goals for yourself, always asking how you can maximize your time and money, and practicing these high-performance habits, you will find yourself immediately living a wealthier life just by being more involved in it. You will always have something to look forward to, something to strive for, and by clearly articulating what you want your future to be, you'll be much more able to live your present.

HEALTH IQ

As you just learned, energy is a high-performance habit; without it, you won't have the fuel to reach your goals. "The higher your energy level, the more efficient your body, the better you feel, and the more you will use your talent to produce outstanding results." That's a quote from Tony Robbins that encapsulates why developing your Health IQ is as essential a step to building real wealth as either of the other two IQ toolkits. I don't care how good you are with money or how well you think about your life: if you don't have the stamina and drive to use your skills, you won't get very far.

The mind is an organ of the body, and like all your other organs, it works better the healthier you are. A bulk of traditional Western thought suggests that the mind and body are separate, but whose experience does this reflect? Every single person I know reports having more focus, sharper thoughts, and a better attitude the more they exercise. Health is what you are going to build all these other habits and ways of thinking on. Most people want to ignore their health as long as they can, and if you're one of those people, let this be your wake-up call to get healthy now.

Developing your Health IQ requires a different approach to wellness than most of us are taught growing up. Most Americans will only go to the doctor when they are feeling bad or when something acute is hurting them. Our entire healthcare insurance system is set up around this idea. When we go to the doctor, they'll charge us à la carte for our various ailments and their specific diagnostic procedures. This method works fine for emergencies, when something needs to be treated right away, but very often by the time we end up going to the doctor, the problem has already grown so large that the solution will be entirely disruptive—if it's not too late.

Integrative medicine and its teachings are an essential part of the Wealth IQ toolkit: it's the holistic wealth strategy of healthcare. Instead of looking at one symptom or issue, integrative doctors view the entire person—their lifestyle, their genetics, their diet, and exercise plans—and make assessments and observations from this whole picture. The philosophy behind integrative medicine is to identify and anticipate illness or disease well before they become a serious problem.

Recently my doctor informed me that my ferritin levels were too low. Ferritin is a blood protein that contains iron—it's vital for carrying oxygen to all the different parts of your body.

This is a common problem among people who work out often, so I wasn't surprised that my tests gave cause for concern. I exercise every day, and I certainly didn't feel bad at all when I went to see my doctor, but had he not practiced integrative medicine, I only would have learned about my low levels of ferritin after it was too late. Because I take an integrative approach to my health, I was able to adjust my daily habits accordingly to accommodate this new obstacle.

Like everything else I advocate for in this book, an integrative approach to health, and thus a robust Health IQ, empowers you to take an active role in your life. With a traditional medical approach, you will be running into health issues only when you have to act on them immediately. That's more time spent in the hospital or recovery and more time on an extensive cocktail of medication. With an integrative approach, you can easily check in on the picture of your health and make your own decisions about how to improve it, well before you "have" to do anything.

Most people do not approach their health this way. They might exercise, they might eat their veggies, but they mostly follow general health advice (if they follow any). This is similar to the way most people follow the traditional roadmap to success without thinking about their own goals and unique financial situation. Your health is as important as it is specific to you: your strategy for leading a healthy life should be equally important and specific.

Beyond integrative medicine, the other key aspect of a strong Health IQ is the practice of creating lifelong goals. Just like you set goals for your wealth and lifestyle, you should set goals for your health. I don't just mean certain amounts you want to be able to bench press or miles you can run: I mean features of your life in the future that only a healthy way of living can provide you. Doctor Peter Attia frames longevity goals as training for the centenarian Olympics. So if you want to be picking up your grandchildren and be able to put your luggage overhead on a plane in your last decade, then what goals do you need to create for yourself today in order to get there?

THE BOTTOM LINE: YOU ARE YOUR BIGGEST ASSET

LeBron James spends $1.5 million a year on his body. It's almost impossible to imagine spending that much money on just your health, but you can certainly conceive of how someone who makes his living from his body might be incentivized to spend that much. You don't need to be the best basketball player in the world to invest in yourself, however. Though you probably don't need to spend quite that much on your own health, you do need to begin viewing these kinds of financial decisions as an investment instead of an expense.

Earlier, I said I want to live to 116—that's my longevity goal. I also have a vitality goal of *how* I want to live to 116. I want to stay active and strong throughout that entire period, being able to pick up my grandkids and go swimming and biking with them. If the choice is between 116 in a wheelchair and nasal tubes or eighty and the picture of health, I know which option I'm taking. Because I take an active role in setting my lifelong health goals, I feel confident that I can live both a long and healthy life. Getting there requires due diligence, but it's worth that time and money because I'm spending that money on something that won't disappear in my lifetime: I'm investing it in myself.

I also spend a significant amount every year on my business coach, my CPA, and my integrative doctor, but I don't feel bad at all about spending that money because I know it's an investment in me. We are each individually our biggest assets. No matter how big of a number you have in your bank account, your capacity will ultimately be determined by your own abilities and your investment in them. If you can develop the Three Foundational IQs, you will compound your individual value exponentially. Money comes and goes, but you're stuck with yourself for life; as long as you're stuck with yourself, you might as well do everything you can to become the best version of whoever that is.

You've now learned quite a lot about how to improve your personal abilities and think more critically about the life you want to lead. With this foundation firmly set, it's time to learn how to make a holistic wealth strategy. I'll teach you how to minimize your taxes, plan your estate, build a portfolio of alternative investments, and institute your own policy of infinite banking in the next chapter. If you've been paying close attention and integrating the lessons of the past five chapters into your life, you are supremely well equipped to begin making the logistical moves to build real wealth.

Chapter 6

PHASE 3: CREATING A WEALTH INFRASTRUCTURE

BEFORE YOU MOVE IN, YOU HAVE TO MAKE SURE THE WATER'S RUNNING

My first consulting business experienced significant growth in its first few years, so much so that we won the Inc. 5000 Award. Once we got past the early years of investing in the business, our EBITDA shot up, and we felt that everything was good. Our clients were happy, our income looked strong, and we were rapidly scaling the business—we had momentum and the resources to act on it. Then March came around, and we were informed that we'd have a large six-figure tax bill to pay. All of us were shocked. We had the funds to cover the bill, but the sudden revelation that we'd have to pay so much in taxes squashed our energy and the ambitious plans we had for the new year.

Especially when you're running a business, finding out in

March or April that you owe upwards of a quarter of your income in taxes is totally destructive to your finances and your sense of growth. Even if you can manage the amount, finding out so late in the game crushes wealth generation and causes a huge amount of stress.

After years of paying significant, unexpected taxes, I was determined to find another way. I fired a total of four different tax firms before I found a team of CPAs I was actually happy with.

I looked so long for the right CPA because I knew that I needed to take an active approach to my finances. The first four firms I worked with were only able to give me reactive advice that always kept me a few steps behind my money. In this chapter, I'm going to show you how to develop a wealth infrastructure that positions you to take control of your wealth. You can think of a wealth infrastructure like the plumbing and electrical wiring in a house—it's what makes everything else run. You can have the best, most meticulously designed house in the world, but if the water doesn't work, no one will want to live there. Before we get into investments and wealth repositioning, you need to set up a financial foundation that can grow your wealth. When done together, these strategies will protect and grow your wealth in ways traditional financial advice can only dream of.

To build your wealth infrastructure, I'll teach you how to utilize infinite banking, reduce your taxes, plan your estate, and assemble a crack team of experts that will help you achieve your goals. Once you learn how to practice these strategies, you will have developed a wealth infrastructure that makes you an active participant in your financial future.

LEARNING &
TEAM BUILDING

YOU

TAX STRATEGY
INFINITE BANKING
ESTATE PLANNING

- Reduce your
  biggest expense

- Become your
  own bank

MINDSET

FINANCIAL IQ
MINDSET IQ
HEALTH IQ

- Invest in yourself

- Your Why

- Challenge existing
  biases

- Build a fortress
  around your
  wealth & family

- Growth
  Mindset

- Learn new
  strategies

- Build your
  Dream Team

- Beliefs

- Health

- Habits

- Goals

VISION STATEMENT

The same year our consulting business was walloped with unexpected taxes, we were also caught off guard by something called government sequestration, which was a cease on all government spending that put a halt to all of our government contracts overnight. A few things happened in rapid succession, and within ninety days we went from receiving the Inc. 5000 award to facing a half million in debt. I had the flexibility to form a cash flow cushion and manage expenses, but trying to get the bank to expand our loan when we needed it the most was a nightmare. We had to collateralize everything, putting us in a very precarious situation. It was a scary, unstable time that was made worse by the rigid compliance of traditional financial institutions. Had I known about infinite banking, that entire crisis would have been avoided.

Now that your curiosity is piqued, it's time to break down what infinite banking actually is. Infinite banking is a series of financial processes and practices developed by Nelson Nash that empower you to become your own bank. With an infinite banking policy in place, you won't go to a traditional bank when you need to generate liquidity; instead, you'll go to yourself. If this intimidates you, it shouldn't—this is actually a strategy that ultra-wealthy families and family offices have been using for decades as the cornerstone to their wealth strategies.

To start infinite banking, you establish a properly structured dividend-paying whole life insurance policy with a cash value to it. Over time, you can continue to contribute to it, and in turn, create more value. Since it's a life insurance policy, the cash inside of it grows completely tax (including compound tax) free. You can also then transfer the money in it to your heirs completely tax-free and without probate.

Whenever you need money, you can simply take out a loan against this policy. You don't need to be a business or an accredited investor to do this, either—you just need to build up that initial life insurance policy. That is the core of the infinite banking policy. It's very simple, but it is one of the best ways for an individual to add liquidity, protection, and velocity to their wealth.

As you begin accumulating the cash value in your policy over time, not only can you leverage the principal for cash reserves or investments in private equity, but you can also create a tax-free income stream in your later years. Since you are building cash value over time, you can withdraw a certain amount per month that is considered a loan against the policy and therefore has no tax liability tied to it. Additionally, the policy is structured so that the cash value is always performing above the projected amount that you withdraw so you can never outlive your money. This is contrary to Wall Street's thesis of accumulation theory that factors in a life expectancy and carries the risk that you may outlive your money.

Many of us have limiting beliefs about loans and think that, no matter what, they are dangerous, unstable, and the source of financial insolvency. Loans can be dangerous, but they aren't if you take them out responsibly and use them to generate more wealth than you initially took as the loan. In the final chapter, I'll take you through ways you can use that cash to create wealth, but the basis of my advice assumes that you are able to begin infinite banking and generate enough money to make impactful investments. If you have limiting beliefs about debt, you need to expand your learning and come to understand better what debt really is and how you can take advantage of it.

Here is how you can generate an almost limitless amount of new money by using infinite banking. The money in your life insurance plan appreciates at a pretty low rate on its own, about 5.5 percent. That's not nothing, but the real way to make money off a life insurance policy is to position the money you borrow against it into other low-risk investments such as multifamily real estate syndications. Any time you want to generate a bit more passive income, stop by your infinite bank, make a loan against your policy, and invest that money into multifamily real estate or similar opportunities. With the expected 20 percent return and the 5.5 percent appreciation, you will be more than able to cover the costs of the loan while generating a backflow of cash that you can use to increase the initial life insurance policy and add significant velocity to your overall wealth. This is the magic of how you can use the same dollar twice, and it's probably the most powerful tool you can have in your wealth management toolkit.

If you have a net worth of $15 million or more, you can even take advantage of something called premium financing which allows you to partner with a bank that actually pays your premiums on a significant policy and still yields all the benefits outlined.

THE SECURITY AND EFFICIENCY OF AN INFINITE BANK

One of the great advantages of securing your funds in a life insurance policy is that it has inherent asset protection. If something horrible happened, like you or a loved one got into a car accident and someone tried to sue you, the first place they are going to look for liquidity is in your stock accounts and your house. While money tied up in personal real estate or the stock market is susceptible to these kinds of financial attacks, your life insurance policy is totally protected: it's life insurance, so a claimant would have a very hard time going after it. That layer of asset protection is essential to feeling confident that your investments are safe from the inherent unpredictability of life.

Whatever you build with your wealth, you need to ensure that it is on a stable base of cash liquidity. Your life insurance policy will become that foundation. The well-trod path to success advises you to put any large-scale earnings into Wall Street or possibly a retirement account, but instead, you'll dump that cash back into the beating heart of your infinite banking policy. Once it's there, it'll passively generate about 5.5 percent in tax-free income while giving you a bigger cushion to loan against. This is where you want to keep your year's reserve of living expenses. This money doesn't care if the stock market is up or down: it's completely stable and safe where it is.

When my wife and I bought a second house in Florida, we didn't have to wait around at all for a bank to raise the cash or deal with an onerous bank loan application—we just tapped into our life insurance policy and took out the $150,000 we needed for the down payment within a few days. I borrowed against that deposit and was then able to set up my own terms to pay it back when it worked for me.

That's the power of liquidity: it allows you to make these big, life-changing financial moves without having to wait around for anyone else. As much as you might intuitively agree with the adage of "buy low, sell high," it's impossible to enact if you don't have the liquid cash lying around. Plenty of people have massive piles of money locked away in their personal residences or the stock market that are sizable but completely immobilized. What is the point of having that much money if you can't access it when you really need it? I would also argue that capital invested in equities isn't always as liquid as it seems. When you need capital it may not always coincide with whether your equity positions are up or down, and no one likes selling when you are down. Infinite banking is the way you are going to turn your wealth into something pliant enough to actually use and generate velocity with your wealth.

There isn't really a downside to infinite banking, but you do need to set up your life insurance policy in a very specific way to get it started. If you were to call up an insurance company and tell them what you wanted to do with your life insurance policy, they probably wouldn't really understand how to help you. Insurance agents can also send you down the wrong track, as they are incentivized to set up a policy that generates the largest commission for them—which just so happens to be the opposite structure of what works for infinite banking. I don't expect you to be an insurance specialist, so you will need to include someone in your financial team who can set this up. That's a big part of why we wanted to offer infinite banking as a solution at Pantheon: we wanted to create value for our clients by being able to set this up as the foundation to their wealth strategy for ultimate liquidity, tax efficiency, safety, and velocity.

> To schedule a free consultation and determine if infinite banking is right for you go to: https://pantheoninvest. com/banking.

TAX STRATEGIES

What's your biggest expense? Housing? Travel? Education? These are the answers I usually get when I ask that question, though none of them are correct. The right answer is: taxes. Everyone's single biggest expense on their income statement is their tax payments, pretty much regardless of their tax bracket. Yet we are not taught to think of them as expenses, but rather an unavoidable fact of life, something that we just have to take on the chin and move past. The people who know that this isn't true? The truly wealthy.

If you want real wealth, you need to change your perspective on taxes and start partnering with the government to take advantage of the incentives they offer the way a wealthy person does. That doesn't mean paying in an exorbitantly high tax bracket; it means understanding how taxes work for business owners and investors and taking advantage of the incentives that are offered.

Tom Wheelwright is a thought leader in the tax management space. He's Robert Kiyosaki's CPA, and he has completely revolutionized the way we conceive of taxes. He sums up his philosophy like this: "if you want to change your tax, change your facts." In practice, this takes many forms, but the core of the idea is that you need to position your assets and sources of income in ways that best take advantage of existing tax incentives.

The tax code is one of the most misunderstood pieces of financial writing out there. Though most people think of it as a series of penalties and fines designed to extract value from you at every twist and turn, the tax code we have in the United States is actually a series of incentives to encourage behaviors beneficial to society and the economy. Some of my clients are squeamish about changing their facts to change their tax, but the truth is that the government actually encourages this kind of tax strategy itself. When we understand that taxes are really incentives, then we can position ourselves to take advantage of them.

One key strategy to reducing your taxes is what's known as income shifting. To shift your income, you want to restructure how income is flowing into your personal economy. One example, as mentioned earlier, would be to give your children a job in your business and pay them wages that will be an expense to you and taxed at their tax rate. They could use that money to save for college versus you taking your top-level wages and then paying for the college savings out of your pocket. Another example would be creating an entity for your small business, which may be taxed at a different rate than your W-2 job and provide you with options to deduct your expenses. That might be a rental property or a small business—anything that you can claim deductions on or possibly hire employees through.

At the beginning of this book, I mentioned that my family and I visit our house in Italy tax-free. We don't live there year-round, so we're able to rent out the property for a couple of months out of the year. Because it's a rental property and we work in the business, we can deduct our flights to and from it from our taxes. Since we have mortgage interest on the property, we also get depreciation on it. We bought the house because it was our vision to truly experience the Italian culture, but because we've positioned it in this way, it's also a source of income for us.

When my wife and I want to give our children some money, we always make sure to pay them through one of our businesses. By distributing wages from those entities, we turn our support for our children into a salary. Because they're in much lower tax brackets, they are able to use the money that we pay them for things like their college tuition, paying a far lower amount on that income than we would. There are other incentives we can take advantage of in this tax strategy as well, such as counting their housing expenses during college as deductions if we create rental property for them.

This is the kind of mindset you need to have around your taxes. In all 6,800 pages of the tax code, there is a large amount of opportunity you can take advantage of to minimize your payments to the government, optimizations the government itself encourages. In the final section of this chapter, I'll talk about assembling a dream team around your wealth—those are the people who precisely will help you get into this kind of mindset. Even before then, you can begin to think about your taxes actively to make the most out of your money.

ESTATE PLANNING & ASSET PROTECTION

It's never too early to start protecting your assets and planning your estate. People often wait until the end of their lives to do this, or maybe at the earliest when they have children. You can never know when something terrible is going to happen, so you should begin thinking about asset protection and your estate right away. Planning your estate is just one of many different layers to a wealth infrastructure, and you can really think of it as another form of asset protection, just one that won't directly affect you in your lifetime. If you can create an active, wealth-generating estate plan now, you can set your family up to have true legacy wealth even if something tragic happens.

The traditional advice about estate planning is geared exclusively toward people satisfied with a middle-class lifestyle. To experience real wealth, you need to form a plan that actually takes into account the kind of lifestyle you want to leave behind. A will is an essential part of this plan, sure, but it's far from the only thing you can do to set your loved ones up for real wealth.

Infinite banking is already a huge part of this kind of planning, as it hinges on a well-maintained and funded life insurance policy. If anything should happen to me, I have a large foundation of liquidity in that policy that avoids state taxes and probate. It can also be transferred directly to my heirs with no tax implications or delays. Even if you take a more conservative approach to how you use your infinite bank, building a nest egg in a whole life insurance policy is a great place to build protected, enduring wealth.

Beyond that, you can create a trust. This is something that the world's wealthiest families do exceptionally well: set up financial structures like family offices that ensure their wealth is used to support their values. When you pass away, you should be thinking about more than just the hard assets you pass on to your children and consider the values and virtues you want to steward in them. A simple way of doing this is setting up rules on the trust that state that, if a grandchild or distant relative wants to use some of the money you leave behind to start a business, the other trustees have to agree to the withdrawal. You certainly could parcel your wealth out to individuals, but this rarely accounts for the unpredictability of life and opens the door to major conflicts between members of your family. By enshrining your wealth in a trust and setting clear rules for how that money can and cannot be used, your trustees have a much more concrete way to understand what it is you intended for your money and how you wanted to use it to help them.

Creating a trust also provides a substantial layer of asset protection. There are different layers of protection to consider based upon your personal situation, such as a Domestic Asset Protection Trust or a Foreign Asset Protection Trust, and concepts such as equity stripping that can create significant protection to your wealth. Let's say you have multiple real estate assets. You can create a trust—an entity—that owns them, like a personal holding company. If creditors come after you or any kind of lawsuit happens involving those properties, the claimants would be suing the trust, not you personally. A trust is removed from the person who created it, as there is a level of anonymity surrounding it that you can't get if something is simply in your name. While a trust is impersonal and distanced, an individual is vulnerable, with a personal residence and perhaps a brokerage account that are each vulnerable to malicious parties. You want to own nothing and control everything. Elon Musk does not have one asset in his empire under his personal name.

The more wealth you accumulate, the more important it becomes to set that wealth up in well-protected entities. When you're growing your wealth at first, when your net worth is still relatively small, it's very unlikely that many people will come after your assets—there's just not that much to go after. But as you grow, you need to manage the risk inherent to having so much wealth in your portfolio. I think of this as building a fortress around your wealth; if you're going to follow these steps to grow it, you need to make sure it can grow safely. The moves I propose you make in this book have the ability to make you a significant amount of money very quickly. The only downside to this is that it can put you in a situation where you have more wealth than you know how to protect. You wouldn't buy a safe four weeks after buying a bar of gold—you'd buy it at the same time. The same is true of building your wealth: start constructing a fortress around your wealth well before it becomes large enough to need protection.

THE DREAM TEAM

I don't believe in going it alone. Even though the most important thing you can do to make real wealth is take control of your money, you don't need to silo yourself; in fact, that directly goes against the teachings of the Growth Mindset.

Building a dream team to support your wealth goals is the final component of the wealth infrastructure. If you don't have a stellar team, your wealth will always be more vulnerable and insecure than if you had it supported by top people. You need to constantly stimulate yourself with new ideas and perspectives, so you need to seek out the people who can bring in those new ways of thinking.

My dream team consists of a business coach, a CPA, a strategic wealth advisor, an infinite banking advisor, an asset protection attorney, a cycling coach, and an integrative doctor. Not on this list are mastermind groups I belong to and people that I have a more informal, but no less valuable, relationship with, like my wife and my best friend Keith. They both give me invaluable advice, and their contributions to my way of thinking cannot be overstated.

Building a dream team takes time. I mentioned earlier that I fired four separate CPAs until I found one that I liked, but I don't regret the time I took to form these relationships around my wealth. Unlike infinite banking or planning your estate, you're not going to assemble your dream team overnight. Nor would you want to: you cannot rush any kind of relationship, and if you try to, you more often than not end up in one you struggle to get out of.

To expedite the process for you, however, I've included a list of referrals to the people that I like to work with. These are the relationships that I've cultivated over the entire course of this obsessive quest for wealth, and these people are truly some of the best in their respective businesses. They may or may not be right for you and how you like to work, but the list that I have curated is an incredible place to start—I wish I had a list like that when I first set out on this journey.

You can access the list here: https://pantheoninvest.com/resources/.

The best thing I can tell you to look out for when you're building your dream team is highly specialized players who are at the top of their game. This is the best indicator of success. With so many options for team members out there, go with the people who support your vision and goals and have the greatest track record of success. It's simple advice, but most people don't center it on their search for a dream team.

As you begin finding members of your dream team, you will be tempted to hire people with the lowest rates. Don't do that. These people are investments, and the more money you invest in them, the more likely they are to give you greater returns. That's not always the case, of course, and you need to carefully evaluate who you are bringing on to your team. Still, you shouldn't cut corners with the people you put around your wealth. If they know what they're doing, they will bring you massive returns on your investment in them, just like any other investment.

A great place to meet members of your dream team is at mastermind groups. Joining these groups and going to their conferences can cost tens of thousands of dollars, but their high cost is actually part of the draw. By setting such a high fee, automatically the vast majority of the population is excluded, leaving you access to the highest earning and most ambitious people. This is another investment, and you have to consider that the cost associated with joining these high-performing groups will be paid back in the unique relationships you can form within them.

The other thing I look for when I'm finding a client a member of their dream team is that they have proven success working with people in the client's goal domain. I highly value my business coach. He's a member of Strategic Coach®, which is an elite coaching group for entrepreneurs specializing in growing their businesses ten times. Business advice is much less generic than you might think—the needs of a $4 million operation are not merely ten times as small as those of a $40 million operation, they actually also require a completely different set of business practices. When you're looking to add someone to your dream team, do some serious research on who that person's clients are. If their clients aren't doing what your objectives are focused on, that advisor is not the right person for you.

THE BOTTOM LINE: A WEALTH INFRASTRUCTURE MAKES YOUR DOLLAR COUNT TWICE

By building a really solid wealth infrastructure, you're able to both grow your wealth and compound it. On the well-trod path to success, you end up immobilizing your money, putting it in complicated and vulnerable financial structures that don't have the strength to empower the growth of real wealth. The common theme among infinite banking, tax reduction, estate planning, and dream team building is stretching your dollar across multiple generative entities. A whole life insurance policy nets you security for your family, and it also gives you the power of liquidity against which you can perpetually take out loans. A dream team helps you form an effective tax strategy and connects you to a network of individuals that you can call to understand your finances better. The power of a wealth infrastructure is its ability to make your dollar work overtime, to position your wealth only in places where it can do many different things at the same time. In order to make the kinds of investments that I advocate for in the next chapter, you need this potent combination of multiplicity and strength.

There were many dynamics that my consulting firm was challenged with, but the biggest one among them was that we lacked a serious wealth infrastructure. We weren't getting the kind of tax advice we needed, and we had only one way to raise liquid funds: the bank and its rigid policies. Because our wealth infrastructure was underdeveloped, our incredible growth in the years before our struggles meant very little. Today, our business has an incredible wealth infrastructure that includes a comprehensive tax plan that moves on incentives, an infinite banking policy that provides liquidity, protection, and velocity, and a team of some of the best financial thinkers that I have had the pleasure to meet. A great wealth infrastructure is the backbone of your portfolio—be intentional in how you develop it.

* * *

Your mind is open, you're expanding your education, and you have a vision and an idea of how you can build scaffolding to support your ambition. Now it's time to generate the wealth that you've done all this hard work toward achieving. In the next phase, I'll teach my years of accumulated tricks and best practices to reposition your money into more liquid assets and entities.

Chapter 7

PHASE 4: TAKE ACTION: ASSET REPOSITIONING

STEPPING OFF THE WELL-TROD PATH TO SUCCESS

TAKE
ACTION

LEARNING &
TEAM BUILDING

ASSET REPOSITIONING
- Convert existing assets to risk-adjusted, higher-performing, predictable, tax-efficient cash flow
- Target IRAs, 401(k)s, home equity

YOU

**TAX STRATEGY
INFINITE BANKING
ESTATE PLANNING**
- Reduce your biggest expense
- Become your own bank
- Build a fortress around your wealth & family
- Build your Dream Team

**FINANCIAL IQ
MINDSET IQ
HEALTH IQ**
- Invest in yourself
- Challenge existing biases
- Learn new strategies

MINDSET
- Your Why
- Growth Mindset
- Beliefs
- Health
- Habits
- Goals

VISION STATEMENT ──────────────────────────────▶

When I broke out of my 401k, I expected to break even on the 10 percent penalty and taxes in about six years. It was a scary decision, but I knew I needed to get back in control of my money and to escape the holding pattern established by government-qualified plans. Through clever asset repositioning, I broke even in half the time. Now I make at least 30 to 50 percent a year on that money, regardless of the stock market, without paying any taxes on it. And most importantly, I have complete control of what happens to it.

Most people have money sitting in equity in their 401ks that does nothing for them. 401ks are susceptible to the caprices of the stock market and the ballooning tax deferment, and the equity associated with personal real estate is essentially trapped. Despite having very little control of their money, the majority of homeowners and business professionals are content with this kind of investing because it's vouched for by the traditional roadmap to success. This money appears safe, and that's enough for most people to willingly put it into stagnant entities that are incapable of growing wealth. Outside of a Growth Mindset, this is enough. But it's not nearly sufficient for you to live a life of extraordinary wealth.

It's time for you to build a portfolio of alternative assets and entities that minimize *your* tax and maximize your returns. Through decades of research, I've identified some of the best, highest-yield investment opportunities that you can pursue right now. In order for you to take full advantage of them, you need to have followed the previous steps in this book to build a holistic financial structure to support this new wealth. The investments I recommend here are the cumulation of everything that's come before in this book, so don't make the mistake of thinking that you can reposition your portfolio without properly setting yourself up for wealth.

REPOSITIONING FUNDS TO BEGIN ALTERNATIVE INVESTING

Most Americans have been told that the best they can do is to slowly pay off their mortgage and then spend all their remaining money through their retirement, ending up with nothing or very little to pass on to their kids. This way of thinking is already much too modest in its ambitions, and that's before considering that, even if you pay off your mortgage, you absolutely will still have many costs associated with keeping up your house.

Before you can make any alternative investments, you need to have the capital to actually invest in the first place. None of the investments I suggest can be done with less than $50,000, though $100,000 is the ideal minimum. If you're on the traditional roadmap to success, you won't be able to see how you could possibly have the money to start these investments. For many people, $50,000 or $100,000 seems like an insurmountable bar to entry—who has that kind of money lying around to invest?

You do. You just might not know it.

As of 2019, the amount of money in IRA assets in the United States totaled $9.7 trillion; 14.7 percent have more than 50 percent equity in their homes. That is a huge amount of wealth that is, effectively, twiddling its thumbs. The money that you have been told is untouchable, the wealth you have been advised to cut yourself off from—that's your ticket to making alternative investments and building real wealth.

If you have money in a 401k, you have the money to begin

alternative investing. If you have money in a 529 plan, you have the money to begin alternative investing. If you have trapped equity in a family home, you can easily take out a line of credit and begin alternative investing. Many people are scared to do any of these things, so they end up cut off from their own wealth. Taking a line of credit out on your house can be intimidating, as can any of these other moves, but if you follow my advice, you'll be able to place it somewhere that it can generate 20 percent or more a year with zero tax implications. You can then use the revenue generated from those savvy investments to easily pay off the loan. From there, you simply repeat the process until you've reached your wealth goals—which can come much quicker than you might expect.

For my own portfolio, I leverage up to 90 percent against my personal residence in credit. With new clients, I usually suggest 80 percent as a more conservative initial number, but I have had clients that go beyond 90 percent. You and your dream team will have to decide what the right number is for you, but the general principle holds true: the more you leverage, the more comes back to you in return. It's all about positioning your precious capital in the safest and highest-yielding assets. If the bank is willing to loan you money at 5 percent and you can get a 20 percent return on your investment, that is an excellent arbitrage play before even factoring in the additional tax offset you will achieve with mortgage interest.

There are other options available to you to reposition your wealth. If you have trapped equity in an IRA, you can shift some of it into a self-directed IRA. The advantage of a self-directed IRA is that you can actually invest that money into real estate, including the kind of multifamily properties that I strongly advocate for.

There's also something called an EQRP, which is functionally very similar to a self-directed IRA but is itself more like an entity or a solo 401k. These aren't my number one favorite ways to generate passive income, but they can be great starting places for the average person to begin wealth repositioning.

HOW CREDIT PROTECTS YOUR MONEY

Conventional wisdom asserts that credit is the most unstable, most dangerous form of capital out there. And that's true, if you use that credit on frivolous things that don't generate any wealth themselves. If you use that credit wisely, however, you can end up leveraging it basically indefinitely to make yourself a huge amount of money. There is another bonus to credit, specifically credit taken out against your personal residence: it actually makes your money much safer from malicious parties.

A very essential tool to protect your money is in what's known as a Home Equity Line of Credit or HELOC. If you take a HELOC against your home, you're essentially telling creditors that this tantalizing asset to them (your house) is mostly owned by the bank. I don't care how much money you have and how many lawyers you're prepared to hire—the bank will always have more money than you and more attorneys to throw at a problem. By taking a HELOC, you actually let the bank use its size and authority to protect your wealth. As "unconventional" as this thinking is, it's actually perfectly logical when you take the time to think about it yourself.

PASSIVE INVESTING THESIS

Just from the money I have invested, I am able to pay for my family's expenses, our travel, even our mortgage payments on several personal properties, entirely from passive income. That's not from some obscenely large number generating fractions of a percent in the stock market; rather, that money comes from high-yield, savvy investments that are geared toward building sustaining income for myself and my family.

Once you get some wealth generated in alternative assets, you will be tempted to purchase what Robert Kiyosaki terms "do-dads." "Do-dads" are liabilities that stagnate your money, that suck it up without providing any opportunities for growth. At the extreme end of things, this could be a private island, but it could also be something much tamer, like a new car or a fancy kitchen. Whatever they actually are, "do-dads" are essentially liabilities that trap cash and potentially threaten the stability of your wealth. You want to get to a point with your wealth where you can purchase these luxuries with the passive income generated from your assets to support your lifestyle, but make no mistake: they are luxuries, not investments.

What you really want to put your money into are cash-flowing tangible assets. A cash-flowing asset is an asset that provides predictable passive income, has tax efficiency, and also provides an opportunity for equity growth through forced appreciation. This enables the passive income you receive to be tax-free, while your equity grows in parallel. The more assets you are able to purchase, the greater you can grow your passive income. I call this widening your base.

Let's say you have $500,000 of trapped equity in your primary residence. If you take a line of credit out against that property at a 5 percent interest rate and put that money in a multifamily real estate syndication, you can easily generate a 7 percent cash flow and see that initial investment appreciate by 10 percent plus a year. Your taxes on the cash flow will be offset by bonus depreciation, and your new LOC will have interest that is deductible, further supporting your tax strategy. With very little effort, you can take your trapped equity and reposition it into something that generates immense passive income and freedom for you and your family.

This is the heart of the passive income investment thesis. You acquire cash-flowing assets that provide tax-free income. Every time you have a liquidity event you buy more assets to keep building your base that keeps increasing your income. Upon purchase, you can take advantage of bonus depreciation of these assets, which provides a paper loss on your asset that offsets the income generated. Once you have enough passive income that exceeds your expenses, you are essentially financially free and don't need to work for a paycheck any longer. Once you can let go of all the traditional financial planning advice and execute this strategy, it becomes a process that you can iterate over and over.

Think about all the freedom this can provide for you by truly achieving Freedom of Money. I know entrepreneurs that have achieved this milestone and have been able to create new businesses of their dreams. I know doctors who have achieved this milestone but continue practicing medicine in an entirely new way that is according to their terms and time frame. I know pilots who have achieved this milestone and are no longer shackled to spending their entire careers flying for an airline.

For me, I am always looking to create a bigger future for myself and my family where my lifestyle needs are always covered by my passive income. What about you? What type of new freedoms could you create by leveraging this strategy?

You won't be able to make any of these investments without an expansive Growth Mindset. In order to live a wealthy life, you need to be constantly looking for ways that you can make your dollar count two, even three times over and get you where you want to go. You want to be thinking in terms of multiples: how fast can I double my money, how fast can I 10x my passive income? How can I double my assets? Wall Street has us all thinking that there is only one ROI (return on investment) to be made with your capital but the top 1 percent know that it's all about creating a multiplier effect where you can enjoy exponential results by accomplishing many returns with the same dollar. If you're thinking of your wealth as something to be hoarded, not grown, then you won't see these opportunities for wealth repositioning.

THE BOTTOM LINE: COUNTERINTUITIVE LOGIC IS HOW YOU'LL REPOSITION YOUR WEALTH

In order to build your wealth, you are going to need to do some things that would make those on the well-trod path to success shudder. This can be an extremely hard step for people to take, especially if they are surrounded by people with limiting beliefs about money. Despite its unpopularity among leading middle-class thinkers, leveraging credit against your home and other wealth repositioning tactics is an essential first step toward building the life you want to live. This is what the ultra-wealthy have been doing for years, and while it might seem like they're only able to do it because of generational wealth, the reality is that you can get yourself on the same path today just by making a few rational, if counterintuitive, financial decisions. You have the money you need to start building your wealth—now it's time to use it as efficiently as possible.

Breaking out of my 401k was one of the best decisions I've made in my life, and everyone I knew told me I was crazy for doing it. The well-trod path to success has a pretty iron grip on how we think about money, so it's no surprise that leaving a government-qualified plan sounds like such a bad idea to so many. But by really thinking about what I was doing, and researching what I could do with all that freed-up money, I realized that leaving my 401k was actually the safest, most sure way I could reach my wealth goals. Just because something is unconventional does not mean that it's a bad idea; in fact, unconventional thinking is usually the only way to get you where you want to go.

* * *

With your wealth repositioned and finally accessible to you, you can begin to use that flexible money to invest in asymmetric low-risk, high-yield, alternative assets. In the next chapter, I'll walk you through some of my favorite alternative assets and how you can quickly and painlessly get your money into them. Once you're aware of the incredible investment opportunities waiting for you out there, you will be stunned no one had told you about them before. With your money finally your own again, you will be able to make investments that generate the massive, passive income you need to live an extraordinary life.

Chapter 8

PHASE 5: BUILDING MASSIVE PASSIVE INCOME

LIVING AN EXPANSIVE LIFESTYLE

TAKE ACTION

LEARNING & TEAM BUILDING

YOU

TAX STRATEGY INFINITE BANKING ESTATE PLANNING
- Reduce your biggest expense
- Become your own bank
- Build a fortress around your wealth & family
- Build your Dream Team

ASSET REPOSITIONING
- Convert existing assets to risk-adjusted, higher-performing, predictable, tax-efficient cash flow
- Target IRAs, 401(k)s, home equity

BUILD MASSIVE PASSIVE INCOME
- Multifamily RE syndications
- Oil & Gas syndications
- Accredited investor syndications
- Side hustle business
- Build a business

FINANCIAL IQ MINDSET IQ HEALTH IQ
- Invest in yourself
- Challenge existing biases
- Learn new strategies

MINDSET
- Your Why
- Growth Mindset
- Beliefs
- Health
- Habits
- Goals

VISION STATEMENT

My personal goal is to have a passive income that always exceeds my lifestyle. For me, this means constantly expanding the way I live, filling my life and the life of my family with richer experiences and more opportunities. To do this, I'm always maximizing my wealth and seeking out new strategies. This enables me to take as much time off work as I want without having to worry about supporting my family. Because my living expenses are covered by my passive income, everything I make from my work goes to building out my investments and increasing the quality of my expansive lifestyle. It's all about expanding your freedom, your experiences, and your relationships.

Many people dream of this kind of abundant life—I certainly did before I started to live it—and they wrongly think that the only way to get there is through brutally hard work and a life of restraint. Books like The Millionaire Next Door advocate that you cut yourself off from anything and everything that you enjoy to reach an arbitrary amount of money that stagnates in a retirement account or the like. Meanwhile, the traditional roadmap to success urges you to spend your whole life reaching a retirement nest egg number by the time you retire just to watch it disappear by the time you pass away. You can do so much better in so much less time.

The key to living an expansive lifestyle is understanding and utilizing passive investment theory. This is the chapter where I will tell you about the crown jewel of personal investment: multifamily real estate syndications. Using these investment opportunities and a few other alternative assets like them, you will be able to generate enough passive income not just to support the bare necessities of life but also to fuel the abundant lifestyle of your dreams.

MULTIFAMILY REAL ESTATE SYNDICATIONS

After the passage of the JOBS Act in 2012, smaller-scale investors were allowed to invest in multimillion dollar properties through crowdfunding. Before it was passed, the investment opportunities I'm discussing were only available to ultra-wealthy individuals who could raise 100 percent of the funds themselves. This act empowered people to come together and form syndications (groups of investors) to pool their money and make a down payment collectively on a great piece of real estate. This has a number of advantages that I'll walk you through, but of course, the best one for you and the average investor is the ability to get a share of a lucrative large-scale rental property without putting up massive amounts of wealth. The buy-in for these kinds of investments is typically at $50,000 at a low minimum or $100,000 ideally—an amount of money you can readily raise using the techniques I discussed in the previous chapter. Of course, you can and should invest more money in these syndications, but this is the bar to entry.

Let's look at these investments in practice. Compare a $100,000 investment in a real estate syndication versus one in a standard, single-family rental property. On the surface, you might think the single-family home is the better option, as you get to own all of it. But what happens when you can't find a renter? Or the renter you do have is behind on their payments? Or the roof needs to be replaced? In any of those instances and many others, your rental income drops to $0. Not only that, you have to keep up with your tenant or hire a property manager—both of which can be massive drains on your time and money.

Compare this to an investment in a real estate syndication.

Among a group of investors, you're one of a number of limited partners on a deal. You'll get access to a completely top-notch asset, like a $50 million, 300-unit apartment building in a rapidly growing area. You'll be buying into an established institution with systems in place to ensure that rent is collected on time, facilities are managed, and tenants are satisfied by a property manager. Through the size and experience of the syndication, you'll also get access to off-market properties and other exclusive opportunities. You won't need to live geographically close to the property, so you won't be limited to the whims of your local housing market. Best of all, you won't have to spend any of your precious time managing the property.

Typically, these investments provide about a 6 to 8 percent annualized cash distribution, tax efficiency, and appreciation gains of 10 percent or more per year for the investors. That's significantly better than what you can expect to do in the stock market, but the benefits don't end there as we have that multiplier effect here. Firstly, that rate of return is generally unaffected by the stock market or even the state of the economy; no matter what's going on in the world, everyone needs a place to live and shelter, one of Maslow's most basic needs. So this asset class possesses a great deal of recession resistance. Secondly, that money is 100 percent passively generated. After you sign your check, you basically don't have to do anything else as a team of experts manage your asset and are incentivized to do so. On a risk-adjusted basis, this asset class is definitely one of the best performing to be at the core of your portfolio.

There are other passive investments you can make: oil and gas, self-storage, car washes, bitcoin mining, hotels, agriculture, and so on. After twenty years of research and investment, I have found that multifamily real estate syndications are the Holy Grail of investing, but no financial planner will tell you about them; in fact, if you ask, they'll probably downplay their profitability. This is because the planner has nothing to gain from you taking your money out of the stock market and putting it in this kind of investment. Remember that this is the only thing that makes this extremely stable and lucrative investment "alternative": the financial advising industry has no interest in you making these kinds of investments.

FORCED APPRECIATION

That 6 to 8 percent cash flow return is just the beginning. Through a process known as forced appreciation, you can also expect to receive anywhere between 12 and 14 percent of your initial investment in annual growth paid out upon exit. The hold period is typically five years for this type of project, and each investment has a forecasted return profile to meet the particular business plan. There is usually a cash flow component as well as an equity component. The general partners are incentivized to meet or exceed the plan and will receive higher compensation if done so. It's typical to see return profiles from 16 to 21 percent. We've even had projects go full cycle that doubled those ranges when the market was strong, and the team executed well, and it's already nearly three times better than what you can do in the stock market all with lower risk.

When a syndication invests in a building, the best thing that a group of investors can do is increase the value of the building. This is forced appreciation. There are a number of ways to do this, but you as a casual investor will not have to lead any of it—this will be handled by the company managing the building. After the purchase, you should go in and renovate the units. Replace the floors, upgrade the appliances, things like that. That right there is enough to reasonably increase the rent by $100 a month. You can also get more creative, and this is where the fun of real estate investing comes in. In some of the buildings I have my clients invest in, they'll add valet trash services, expansive mail rooms, or pet parks. All of these things will increase the overall value of the building and in turn, the amount you can charge for rent, so you can get creative with how the team is going to increase the value of your assets.

You're already getting a certain amount of appreciation just through your initial investment in a property in high job and population growth markets, but by adding features and updates to the building, you're driving up the net operating income, which drives up the valuation of the asset itself. This is because commercial assets are valued on a multiple of the net operating income. After about five years, we'll turn around and sell off those properties, leaving the original investors with the gains from the appreciation and 100 percent of their initial investment. That's how we get to that 16 to 22 percent range I mentioned earlier—all at minimal cost to the investor, both in terms of time and money.

CHANGING DEMOGRAPHICS AND LIFESTYLES

One of the great advantages of investing in multifamily real estate syndications is that it plays off of trends in how Americans live today. Right now, the United States is experiencing a tremendous amount of immigration. When people move to the U.S., what do they first do? They rent. That means there is a huge market for rental properties among a wide variety of price points. In addition to international immigration, there is a huge amount of domestic immigration taking place as well. The coasts, once the end goals for many Americans, are simply becoming too expensive for most people to live. Consequently, we are seeing a massive migration of Americans from places like California and New England to the Southwest and Southeast in particular. Cities like Austin, Dallas, Charlottesville, Phoenix, Greenville, and cities all throughout Florida are experiencing a massive surge of new residents, most of whom are looking for a place they can rent to live. These huge apartment complexes are at the center of American migration—that's where you want your money to be right now.

We also take into account geographic information before making an investment. At Pantheon, we don't invest in buildings in New York or San Francisco because those environments have far too high taxes and aren't landlord friendly enough to actually be appealing. Not to mention that they are experiencing more emigration than immigration—people don't want to live there like they used to. We also avoid places like Las Vegas that have very little diversity of industry. Las Vegas requires tourism to drive up its median income, so when something unexpected happens, like a global pandemic, its economy is left very vulnerable. A city like Dallas, on the other hand, has low taxes and a vibrant economy fueled by many different industries that give it some protection from disaster. Investing in real estate syndications gives us a measure of flexibility in where we want to invest, so we make sure to take full advantage of that before we make an investment.

At the same time, millennials—the most important generational demographic—are rapidly shifting away from home ownership toward the life renting can provide. Millennials more than any other generation want rich experiences and lifestyles that the rigidity of home ownership doesn't offer. Multifamily real estate properties are perfectly poised to take advantage of these trends in behavior, which is a huge part of what makes them so profitable.

STAYING ON THE RIGHT SIDE OF INFLATION

There is no denying that at the time of this writing (2023) we are in an inflationary market. It won't last at such a drastic rate, but it will continue to happen. Any money that people have in the bank is completely susceptible to inflation, and we're all seeing how Wall Street and the Fed respond to it; namely, punishing the consumer. It's more important than ever to secure assets that are protected from high inflation rates. In that regard, multifamily properties are exceptionally secure. With inflation high, the cost of rent and utilities naturally goes up. If you own a building or part of one, you get to benefit from that increase in costs. Multifamily real estate investment is one of the few places that you can actually get on the right side of inflation, providing you with a nice cushion against the insecurity of the dollar.

The other way that these properties utilize inflation is by incurring debt. Many of the properties that we invest in have a certain amount of debt against them—that's part of how we can get them at good rates. Debt is inherently secured against inflation, as it's a cost deferred into the future. Because the value of the dollar is shrinking by the day while the cost of the debt stays the same, you're effectively paying less by paying later. Assets with debt associated are a great way to get around the risk of inflation.

Investor Accreditation

Before you can make any of these investments, however, you have to be an accredited investor. When the JOBS Act was passed, the SEC put this system of accreditation into place to protect individuals from irresponsible investments. To become an accredited investor, you need to have made $200,000 for the last two years, or $300,000 between you and a spouse for the last two years, or have over $1 million in net worth outside of your primary residence. Depending upon how a deal is structured, you also usually need a third-party verification from a CPA to basically validate the accreditation. You can also have this completed through various online firms such as verifyinvestor.com This is the bare minimum you need to get in on many of these syndications, so if you're not yet at these thresholds, you need to do whatever you can to get past them.

ALTERNATIVE ALTERNATIVES

Multifamily real estate syndications will always be the cream of the real asset investment crop, but there are other alternative investments out there that can also yield excellent returns, tax efficiency, and downside protection all in one.

OIL AND GAS

Remember, as part of our investment thesis, we look for assets that are non-correlated to the stock market and also are at the base layer of Maslow's hierarchy. Energy is certainly a basic need. The global demand for energy is only accelerating, and we are a long way from getting to a carbon-zero state. I'm all for reducing global warming but even producing green energy sources, like lithium batteries for electric cars, requires massive amounts of petroleum-based energy to do the mining and produce the batteries that come on the marketplace. Petroleum is used in everything from the shampoo and makeup you use to the packaging for every product you buy on Amazon.

Because of a program initiated in the Reagan era, investments in energy can be up to 100 percent tax deductible. Additionally, you can use this deduction against your active income. That's right, a 100 percent tax deduction against your W-2 income.

The oil and gas industry does have a checkered past but recently went through a down period from the pandemic as oil prices hit rock bottom. As a result, there was no investment in the industry in the past four years, and with demand booming right now, there is a significant opportunity for investment in this space.

Many oil and gas investments in the past were very speculative in nature with a big promise for big returns if oil was recovered. Now, there have been considerable changes in technology that have significantly increased the identification and extraction of oil and gas.

Investing in oil and gas provides a trifecta of investing: tax deduction, strong cash flow, and potential for a lucrative upside by selling assets through divestitures.

SELF-STORAGE PROPERTIES

We are a nation of hoarders. Americans love their stuff, and with the largest generation (baby boomers) rapidly downsizing their homes, there is a revitalized market for storage. Naturally, this has increased the demand for self-storage properties.

Self-storage makes for an excellent alternative investment that shares many positive attributes with multifamily properties. Since people don't tend to suddenly abandon their family heirlooms kept in storage units, these assets are low-risk sources of consistent income. You can use the same depreciation techniques to lower your exposure to tax on them, and you can force their appreciation by increasing safety at your property, improving curb appeal, utilizing extra space on the premises, or really anything else you can think of. The upkeep costs on them are also extremely low—a facility of 500 units can be safely managed by one person. Everywhere you go in the country you can see more and more of these things popping up; this is a hot investment opportunity. It's not the most glamorous investment, but with low expenses, these assets generate solid cash flow and are very recession resistant.

MOBILE HOME PARKS

Mobile home parks are another excellent place to make an investment. Like self-storage facilities, the overhead of running them is very low, since the actual units are owned and operated by the people who live in them. Mobile home parks are basically like apartment buildings without any actual buildings, but the revenue source is the same for you as an investor; instead of renting out the apartments, you rent out the land they are parked on. Many of the existing parks out there are small mom-and-pop operations that typically don't have much in the way of amenities or even up-to-date facilities. That means there is much room for development and thus forced appreciation at these parks. The only downside to this kind of investment is that it's a pretty crowded field for investors right now, so finding an asset you can get in on can be tricky. Even Warren Buffet and other institutions have been gobbling up many of these assets across the country.

SENIOR LIVING FACILITIES

For all the same reasons above, senior living facilities are great investments. Some senior living facilities operate much more like a condominium, where the individuals who live there actually own a share of the property. Most, however, work like any other apartment building with renters. Even more than mobile home parks, these facilities tend to be owned and operated by individuals who don't have the funds to improve the quality of the units. Because of the communal nature of these facilities, there are basically a limitless number of ways to force the appreciation of the building. This could be through building recreation rooms, facilities to support medical services, and even art studios or classrooms. The investments in these kinds of properties go a long way to making them a much nicer environment for people to live in, and you're really doing something good for the community by investing in them. I've seen investor syndications bring on quality asset managers with their investment who totally transform these spaces into something the community there is deeply grateful for. For any investor with a philanthropic eye, you can make a huge difference in people's lives by making solid investments in homes for the elderly.

THE PASSIVE INVESTMENT THESIS

When my firm is securing investments for our clients, we take a multi-dimensional approach to identifying great assets. Our strike zone is always to find investments that are low-risk, tax-efficient, have predictable cash flow, have a potentially lucrative exit, and are non-correlated with the stock market. This all makes intuitive sense, however, investments in stocks, bonds, and mutual funds only yield a one-dimensional return despite the promise of traditional financial advisory firms. They use terms like *dollar cost averaging* and *diversification*, but really those are poor excuses for saying they have no control over the performance of your investment, and they hope that returns will only do one thing: rise. In reality, stocks can go sideways and down. Unlike that industry, however, we're not beholden to any one kind of investment option; by looking past the stock market, we are able to cut out the middleman and find a wealth of direct investment opportunities that are significantly safer and more lucrative than what can be found through Wall Street.

TAX EFFICIENCY AND THE MAGIC OF BONUS DEPRECIATION

Tax-efficient properties are essential to growing your wealth portfolio, but there are also ways to report your income that take advantage of the existing tax code. Let's say you have a $100,000 investment in an apartment building. Up to 80 percent of that initial investment can be reported as a loss. You can then take the cash flow of distributions you are receiving from that property and count it against your loss. If you're making 8 percent a year from it, that's essentially $8,000 in income you are earning tax-free. Better yet, the remaining

$72,000 in losses will carry over to the next year, giving you more room to report against your losses.

Personally, I just had two properties that doubled my initial investment, and all the income I've generated off of them has been tax-free because of the magic of depreciation. Even though my initial investment in those buildings is earning me money and actively being used, the IRS sees it as a loss that can be used for a tax deduction.

INVESTMENTS WITH THE POTENTIAL FOR LUCRATIVE EXITS

When we look for an investment opportunity, we make sure there is plenty of room for forced appreciation. We don't want to go in on a building that already has all the amenities its tenants could possibly need—there's no way to add value to those types of buildings. Instead, we look for completely livable buildings that could use just a little bit more love and attention to really drive their value up. Since they have such high rental fees, it's tempting to invest in the most extraordinary, most expensive buildings out there, but it's actually much better to find a building with potential than it is to find one that is already as good as it can be. That way, you are able to take full advantage of forced appreciation to make the most of your initial investment.

Further, by investing in these buildings, you're potentially improving the quality of the community that will form there. This will give you a lucrative exit on the investment and make the tenants happier. If you add a pet park to a building or a more comprehensive exercise room, you're making the individual apartments more valuable to the people who live there. If you've been in a recently renovated apartment building, you might have noticed that there will be an array of charging stations in the lobby. The chances are that these were put in to increase the net operating income estimate, but they also have an incredibly useful function for the people living and visiting there, as that building—put up in the '80s or '90s—wasn't designed for our modern way of life. The charging stations also create competitiveness against other nearby apartment buildings by offering amenities to prospective tenants, which can increase occupancy. As an investor, your first priority has to be toward generating more revenue, but that does not mean you can't also improve the quality of life of the people who live in your investment properties.

ASSETS UNCORRELATED WITH THE STOCK MARKET

We are only focused on real tangible assets that are uncorrelated to the stock market. A multifamily real estate property is a great example of this. In an apartment building, tenants will sign up for year-long leases. If the stock market crashes overnight—as it does all too frequently—no one in an apartment building is going to pull out of their home. They might ditch their stock market portfolio, but they will at least ride out the rest of the lease. This gives investors plenty of time for the economy to rebound and restabilize.

When I tell people about the security of investing in apartment buildings, their mind always goes to the 2008 Financial Crisis. That's reasonable: that was a recession triggered directly by the real estate market. However, many people don't realize that the losses in real estate investment in the late 2000s were almost exclusively felt in the realm of speculation on single-family homes. Investments in apartments, on the other hand, stayed relatively secure. The default rate on multifamily real estate rentals—that is, the number of people who didn't pay their rent—during the 2008 recession was less than 1 percent. Even during one of the country's worst financial crises, investments in multifamily real estate remained secure and stable.

Investments in apartment buildings also have the laws of supply and demand on their side. Right now, the United States has a housing shortfall of 5 million units. Even if every builder in the United States were put to work building new homes and apartments, it would take over a decade to meet that extraordinary demand. Coupled with the living trends of modern Americans skewing away from home ownership to renting, multifamily real estate is perfectly positioned to capitalize on the incredible demand for housing in this country.

WEALTH = MASS + VELOCITY

You need your wealth to have two things before you can really start to see the snowball effect take place: mass and velocity.

Mass gives you the ability to jump on an investment opportunity in a meaningful way. If I tell you about an incredible real estate deal, it doesn't matter how early you know about it if you've only got $10,000 to invest. Investments work with exponential numbers, so you need to have a significant amount available to you to make the most of excellent opportunities. The more mass you have, the more upside you will realize.

You also need velocity. Velocity is the aggregate of many of the wealth generation techniques I discussed in the previous chapters, like tax efficiency and infinite banking. This refers to the speed of how fast your money is growing and having it accomplish several goals at the same time. The more money you have sitting around in a bank account, the more susceptible you are to all kinds of risks—inflation, lawsuits, taxes, etc. To accelerate your wealth, you need to have a ton of it (mass) that you can mobilize quickly, and that is working for you as efficiently as possible (velocity).

Generate Mass with a Side Hustle

If you want to increase your mass of wealth, you should consider starting a side hustle. Many people don't think they have time to start a business on the side. If that's you, look for another job opportunity that complements your current lifestyle—starting a business doesn't just mean spending eighty hours a week running a restaurant. There are so many different kinds of businesses you can start that you should be able to find something that works for you with relative ease. You can start a franchise, a real estate investment business, and even rent out a room in your house as an Airbnb. I have a client who is a commercial pilot who became an appraiser. He's only in the air three days a week, so that leaves him plenty of time for his side hustle and his familial obligations. He's spun his appraising business into a realty firm, and he now takes all the money from his commissions and puts it directly into investments. Working a side hustle, my client is able to bulk up his investment portfolio while gaining greater tax efficiency than he'd have if he were just a W-2 employee.

If you want to move the needle with your investments, you

need to work with as large a mass of wealth as possible. You can certainly start investing with what you have, but you also have to look for opportunities to make more impactful investments with more money to see greater results. Starting a side hustle is a great way to generate the mass you need to start living an abundant life.

THE BOTTOM LINE: YOUR MONEY GOES SO MUCH FARTHER IN ALTERNATIVE INVESTMENTS

Tying it together

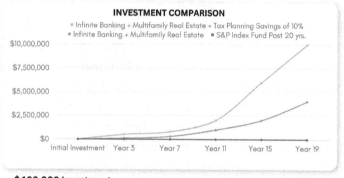

INVESTMENT COMPARISON

- Infinite Banking + Multifamily Real Estate + Tax Planning Savings of 10%
- Infinite Banking + Multifamily Real Estate
- S&P Index Fund Past 20 yrs.

$ 100,000 Investment
- S & P @ 6.16% = $182k
- IBC + RE Syndications @ 20% = $548k
- IBC + Syndications + Tax Savings @ 10% = $1.126M

These kinds of investments are so much more powerful than the returns you can expect from the stock market. When you factor in the tax efficiency, inflation protection, and all the other benefits, you can see how much surer a thing alternative investments are to their supposedly stable counterparts. If you put $100,000 in the stock market, that's it—you have $100,000 of stock. It might go up, it might go down, it will depreciate with inflation, and it's susceptible to all manner of world events. If you take that same $100,000 and put it into multifamily real estate syndication, you end up with a tangible asset that has inherent value. The cash flow from it is protected from taxes and relatively generous, the money you used to invest in it from an infinite banking policy has a little bit of spread to it, and you're able to turn around and cash out that property, which will get you back your initial investment plus appreciation. The advantages to this kind of investment are overwhelming when you compare them to the rigidity of the stock market. Put all of this together and you are regularly looking at a 20 to 30 percent return on investment. And that's a conservative estimate: many of my clients and I regularly do better than that. This is where you want to put your money. This is where you can get it to really work for you.

* * *

This year is my wife and I's twenty-fifth anniversary. To celebrate, we're going on a special vacation to Sardinia. Neither of us has to worry about getting time off or having the money to go; instead, we imagined a dream vacation for ourselves and knew that, through our investments, we'd be more than capable of taking it. This is what massive passive wealth looks like. It goes all the way back to The Four Freedoms™, to this idea that your money should let you live whatever kind of life you want. Because of our investments in multifamily real estate syndications and other alternative opportunities, we're able to lead a life as expansive as we can imagine. If you make investments like these in the way that I suggest, you'll be able to find the same kind of abundant lifestyle.

Now that you know how to think about your money, how to make it work for you, and where to invest it, I want to show you the extent of what a holistic wealth strategy can get you. I'll take you through how I live my life now and how this kind of wealth building has empowered me to live the vision I've set for myself.

Chapter 9

CASE STUDY

LIVING YOUR VISION

I've been on this obsessive quest for wealth for nearly two decades now. It's taken much research and hard work to get to the point that I'm at, but because of all that I've learned about taxes, investing, wealth, and mindset development, I'm living my vision. Using what I've taught you, you can too.

Now you have all the tools you need. To give you a sense of how you can use them, I'll show you how I came to live my personal goal. Your path to an abundant lifestyle will be different, if only because of the fact that your life will be different from mine. However, by looking at how I formed my vision for myself and executed on it, you can get an idea of how you'll do the same.

THE GOAL BEHIND IT ALL

My wife and I have always had a dream of living in Italy. We wanted to truly experience the culture and not just be tourists traveling through. My wife has roots there, and she's always been interested in exploring that part of her heritage. I'm not Italian myself, but I've always been entranced by the European lifestyle and culture. Italy feels authentic to me, the people are so genuine, and it's a place much more directly connected to the everyday experiences of life.

I'm also a huge cyclist, and it doesn't get much better for cycling than in Italy. I'm a member of the largest amateur cycling team in Italy and race and ride with Italians that have become some of my closest friends. The scenery and history are jaw-dropping; from going up switchbacks on the mountains, to stopping for espresso in quaint little villages, to cruising along the Mediterranean Sea, this country is simply awe-inspiring.

We didn't just want to visit Italy—we wanted to live there and learn the language. I've traveled to six continents and over forty countries, so I know that there's a big difference between going to a place and actually being a part of it. My wife and I had no interest in being tourists, or even summer folk; we wanted to live in Italy and experience it the way a native person would.

That's always been our goal, and it's a big part of what's driven me on this quest for real wealth. Because I've had such a clear and ambitious goal this whole time, it's been easier for me to stay on track. This goes all the way back to the importance of dreaming freely; if you're not building toward something really exciting, you're going to run out of the energy you need to get where you want to go.

Eventually, we found a town in Italy that was perfect for us but acquiring real estate there wouldn't be cheap. I had to look for wealth opportunities much more ambitious than I could find on the well-trod path to success in order to make that dream locale a reality. This was about fifteen years ago when my quest for real wealth took off. Despite the scope of our ambitions, we were able to secure the money for that property within a few years. And those weren't five years of scrimping and saving; rather, that was time spent actively building wealth as prescribed in this book.

Once I had learned about multifamily properties and real estate syndications, I located an apartment complex in New Mexico that I and a group of investors went in on. I was able to get enough cash flow from that asset in the first few years to pay the mortgage on the property in Italy. I did this through the exact methods I explained above; I raised the funds for the initial investment through an infinite banking policy I had set up; the general partners forced the appreciation of the building by upgrading its facilities and adding new amenities; I economized my tax payments through depreciation; and finally, after we'd closed on the Italy property, I sold the multifamily building in New Mexico for a huge profit, getting all that initial investment back into my life insurance policy, against which I can generate more liquid cash and start the process all over again. Even better, because we rent out the Italy property when we're not there, I can classify it as a rental asset and deduct all of my family's airfare to and from it as visits to the property. I'm able to use the mortgage interest as a deduction on my taxes here in the States, and I'll only ever pay Italian taxes if I sell the property—which my family and I have no plans of doing.

Because of the way that I've developed my Financial IQ, I've turned my wife and my dream of living in Italy into another wealth-generating, tax-reducing asset. There's a limiting belief out there that the things we spend our money on have to be counted up as losses. That's true for some assets—the "do-dads" that Robert Kiyosaki refers to—but there are a wealth of assets out there that both deliver incredible experiences and bulk up your investment portfolio.

I've also been able to pass on this Financial IQ to my kids. As we set up the Italy property, I taught all four of my children about this kind of real estate investing. My kids were involved in the renovation and development of the Italy property, and they got to learn firsthand how to smartly invest in real estate. My oldest, at just twenty-three, has already bought her first rental property, using the skills my wife and I taught her to build an incredible portfolio at a young age. Since they don't teach these skills at any college or university, that's an education she wouldn't get anywhere else. I'm so excited to see what she does with it.

Now that we've been in Italy for a little over ten years and have purchased three properties, my wife and I also made it a goal to learn the language. Through that, we've met incredible people there who have become our dear friends and who expand our way of looking at the world. We eat, live, and talk like the locals, and we get to share these amazing experiences with our children.

And that's just the beginning. Domestically, we're getting settled in a new home in Florida while we invest in more alternative investment opportunities around the country. Each move we make toward a richer life increases the size of our balance sheet. At the beginning of this book, I talked about how, before I learned to enact a holistic wealth strategy, I always felt like I couldn't keep my head above the ever-rising costs of living. I basically live the opposite of that now; if anything, I struggle to expand the quality of my life to reach the ever-growing profits of my wealth. That is a wonderful problem to have.

THE BOTTOM LINE: IT STARTS WITH YOUR DREAM

There were many steps I had to take in order to create this vision my wife and I had for ourselves, but the very first step was to dream big. None of this would have happened had she and I not had an expansive, ambitious, and wonderful vision for our life. Now that you've read this book, you have all the tools you need to enact your own vision. Take the time to make sure it's a really excellent one.

If you do the research and put in the work, you can live your vision too. There are many ways to gain real wealth, but the holistic wealth strategy that I have developed and shared with you in this book is the quickest, surest, and most sustainable way to get there. As long as you bolster these lessons with new and challenging ideas, as long as you are always keeping your mind open, and as long as you are constantly positioning your wealth to work for you and not the other way around, you will be able to reach any financial goal you set for yourself.

* * *

To wrap up, I'll take you through all the things you've learned over the course of this book. We've covered much ground, and there's no way you can remember everything that I've taught you. You'll likely want to return to specific sections as you begin your own obsessive quest for wealth—use the conclusion as a cheat sheet to get you where you need to go. Soon enough, these behaviors will become second nature, but for now, make sure you really understand each section of the holistic wealth strategy as you begin to implement it in your own life.

CONCLUSION

This book will help you take back control of your money and your life. On this route to financial freedom, wealth is holistic. It's the culmination of a series of investments—both in external assets and in internal development—that empowers an abundant lifestyle. It's the natural extension of your vision for yourself and your mindset, and it's only limited by your capacity to imagine something great. I hope that you make a significant amount of money following my advice in this book, and if you really paid attention to what I shared with you, you're going to. But more than that, I hope this book helps you lead a fuller life. A life where you're constantly challenging and pushing yourself to learn and experience new things. That's what the holistic wealth strategy is for: getting you in control and on the path to an extraordinary life.

LET'S RECAP

The first thing you should do to get back in control is really to take responsibility for your own wealth. The average American spends more time planning their summer vacation than they do their financial future, leaving this most essential feature of modern life in the disinterested hands of a financial advisor. Only after that will you be able to move past the Three Wealth Disrupters and think critically about how you're going to grow your money.

There are many financial systems in place that are designed to keep you from accessing the extent of your wealth, and you need to have the critical thinking skills developed to assess what they are. You also have to dream freely. Without an expansive dream, you will never have an expansive life of your own making.

You have to ensure that you fill life with growth and learning. You need to constantly stimulate yourself with new ideas and new perspectives to put yourself in the driver's seat. The more you invest in your personal growth, the more you grow yourself as your most valuable asset. By developing your Financial, Mindset, and Health IQs, you can build yourself out as an extremely profitable part of your portfolio. Regardless of how the numbers change, this internal development will help you stay in control of your life. Then you can make a wealth infrastructure that will set you up for continued success and agency.

With a wealth infrastructure in place, you'll be much more able to critically assess the kinds of investments and strategies that will get you to the life you want. Many of these ideas exist well outside of the traditional roadmap to success, so you'll need to think broadly in order to access them.

After that, you can begin making alternative investments that net you a much higher rate of return in a much shorter amount of time. By implementing all of these strategies, you'll arrive at a free and abundant life.

THE TIME TO LIVE ABUNDANTLY IS NOW

If you're ready to start living a truly wealthy life, give Pantheon a call. We're here specifically for people like you—people excited to get off the well-trod path to success but who aren't quite sure of the steps to take to get started.

We also have an investor club of like-minded high performers, which you can subscribe to at this link: https://pantheoninvest.com/investor-signup/.

At the end of this chapter, you'll find a link to the Pantheon Learning Center, where you can look at all the materials that I've gathered in my twenty years of experience and research. We're ready and excited to help you start your journey to a better life. We hope you are, too.

How many stories have you heard where someone has to go through something tragic—a loss of a loved one, a chronic illness, a car accident—to get the lightbulb to turn on and get them to take control of their future?

As I began my obsessive quest for wealth, I lived and breathed these stories, trying to understand what I needed to do to get in control. I didn't want to have to go through something traumatizing to get myself where I wanted to be. It took me thousands of hours of reading and listening for the ideas I've developed at Pantheon and beyond to really sink in for me; with what you know now, it doesn't have to take you nearly that long. Ultimately, I wrote this book to get you started. Don't wait for that terrible *something* to happen. This is your lightbulb turning on. Take control of your life now.

ABOUT THE AUTHOR

DAVE WOLCOTT started his career serving the country as a Captain in the Marine Corps. In 2000 he and his wife won the baby lottery having triplets, which inspired him to challenge the traditional financial planning advice of Wall Street. He then started an obsessive journey to understand how the top 1 percent were building their wealth.

A serial entrepreneur at heart, Dave spent the next twenty years building several businesses, investing in alternative assets and creating the Pantheon Holistic Wealth Strategy: the playbook to becoming ultra-wealthy and having not only Freedom of Money, but Freedom of Purpose, Time, and Relationship.

Today, Dave is the Founder and CEO of Pantheon Investments and is more passionate than ever about helping entrepreneurs build wealth by passively investing in superior real estate and alternative assets that provide predictable cash flow, tax efficiency, and upside potential as a reliable alternative to the volatility of the stock market. Dave is also the host of the popular *Wealth Strategy Secrets of the Ultra-Wealthy* podcast and has been a featured guest on numerous media outlets.

ACKNOWLEDGMENTS

I am eternally grateful to my amazing wife, Kristine, and our precious children, Adelaide, John, Claire, and Oliver, who give me life's nectar that is so incredibly fulfilling. Through all the tears and joys you give me my why and inspire me to continue creating even bigger experiences with a future that is always greater than the past.

To all of my investors who hold me to the highest level of accountability with their life's savings: your fears and successes inspire me to solve complex problems and create purpose-driven solutions to minimize your fears, take advantage of your biggest opportunities, and double down on your most important strengths. I am honored to be sharing your journey together to achieve your biggest vision.

CPSIA information can be obtained
at www.ICGtesting.com
Printed in the USA
LVHW101222280423
745513LV00015B/803/J